First World War
and Army of Occupation
War Diary
France, Belgium and Germany

3 DIVISION
Divisional Troops
438 (Cheshire) Field Company Royal Engineers
1 December 1914 - 30 October 1919

WO95/1403/3

The Naval & Military Press Ltd
www.nmarchive.com
Published in association with The National Archives

Published by

The Naval & Military Press Ltd

Unit 10 Ridgewood Industrial Park,

Uckfield, East Sussex,

TN22 5QE England

Tel: +44 (0) 1825 749494

www.naval-military-press.com

www.nmarchive.com

This diary has been reprinted in facsimile from the original. Any imperfections are inevitably reproduced and the quality may fall short of modern type and cartographic standards.

© Crown Copyright
Images reproduced by permission of The National Archives, London, England, 2015.

Contents

Document type	Place/Title	Date From	Date To
Heading	WO95/1403/3		
Heading	2nd Division War Diaries 1/1st Cheshire Field Coy R.E Dec 1914 To December 1916		
Heading	3rd Div R.E., Cheshire Field Coy., Jan-Dec., 1915		
Miscellaneous	1/1 Cheshires F.Coy		
War Diary		01/12/1914	31/12/1914
Heading	III Div Army Troops 121/4610 Cheshire Field Coy. RE (T) Vol I 1.1.15-28.2.15		
War Diary	La Clytte	01/01/1915	28/02/1915
Heading	121/4940 3rd Division Cheshire Field Coy RE Vol II 1-31.3.15		
War Diary	La Clytte	01/03/1915	31/03/1915
Heading	121/5252 3rd Division Cheshire Field Coy RE Vol III 1-30.4.15		
War Diary	La Clytte	01/04/1915	30/04/1915
Heading	121/5775 3rd Division Cheshire Field Coy RE Vol IV 1-31.5.15		
War Diary	La Clytte	01/05/1915	26/05/1915
War Diary	La Clytte & Ypres	27/05/1916	27/05/1916
War Diary	Ypres	28/05/1915	31/05/1915
Heading	121/6063 3rd Division Cheshire Field Coy RE Vol V 1-30.6.15		
War Diary	Ypres	01/06/1915	30/06/1915
Heading	121/6357 3rd Division Cheshire Field Coy RE Vol VI July 15		
War Diary	Ypres	01/07/1915	31/07/1915
Heading	121/6598 3rd Division 1/1 Cheshire Field Coy RE Coy VII From 1-31.8.15		
War Diary		01/08/1915	06/08/1915
War Diary	Sheet No. 2	07/08/1915	10/08/1915
War Diary	Sheet No. 3	11/08/1915	14/08/1915
War Diary	Sheet No. 4	15/08/1915	19/08/1915
War Diary	Sheet No. 5	20/08/1915	27/08/1915
War Diary	Sheet No. 6	30/08/1915	31/08/1915
Heading	121/7082 3rd Division 1/1 Cheshire Field Co. R E Vol VIII Sept 15		
War Diary	The Field	01/09/1915	10/09/1915
War Diary	Sheet No. 2	11/09/1915	17/09/1915
War Diary	Sheet No. 3	18/09/1915	24/09/1915
War Diary	Sheet No. 4	24/09/1915	25/09/1915
War Diary	Sheet No. 5	25/09/1915	25/09/1915
War Diary	Sheet No. 6	25/09/1915	25/09/1915
War Diary	Sheet No. 7	25/09/1915	30/09/1915
Heading	121/7437 3rd Division 1/1 Cheshire Field Coy RE Oct 1915 Vol IX		
War Diary	Sheet No. 1	01/10/1915	05/10/1915
War Diary	Sheet No. 2	06/10/1915	31/10/1915
Heading	121/7663 3rd Division 1/1 Cheshire Field Co. R.E Nov Vol X		
War Diary		01/11/1915	30/11/1915

Type	Description	From	To
Heading	3rd Div Cheshire Fd. Co R.E Dec Vol XI		
War Diary	Ypres (St. Eloi)	01/12/1915	31/12/1915
Heading	3rd Divisional Engineers 1/1st Cheshire Field Company R.E. January 1916		
War Diary	Ypres (St. Eloi)	01/01/1916	31/01/1916
Heading	3rd Divisional Engineers 1/1st Cheshire Field Company R.E. February 1916		
War Diary	Ypres (St Eloi)	01/02/1916	05/02/1916
War Diary	Ypres (St Eloi) And Rest Area (Monecrol)	06/02/1916	09/02/1916
War Diary	Rest Area Monecove	10/02/1916	29/02/1916
Heading	3rd Divisional Engineers 1/1st Cheshire Field Company R.E. March 1916		
War Diary	Rest Area Monnecove	01/03/1916	06/03/1916
War Diary	Ypres (The Bluff)	07/03/1916	08/03/1916
War Diary	The Bluff	09/03/1916	11/03/1916
War Diary	Ypres (St. Eloi)	12/03/1916	31/03/1916
Heading	3rd Divisional Engineers 1/1st Cheshire Field Company R.E. April 1916		
War Diary	St Eloi	01/04/1916	04/04/1916
War Diary	Mont Des Cats	05/04/1916	18/04/1916
War Diary	Vierstraat	19/04/1916	30/04/1916
Heading	3rd Divisional Engineers 1/1st Cheshire Field Company R.E. May 1916		
War Diary	Vierstraat Area	01/05/1916	28/05/1916
War Diary	Rest Area	29/05/1916	31/05/1916
Heading	3rd Divisional Engineers 1/1st Cheshire Field Company R.E. June 1916		
War Diary	Rest Area Mont. De. Cat	01/06/1916	02/06/1916
War Diary	Sherpenberg	03/06/1916	18/06/1916
War Diary	Oaterzeele	18/06/1916	18/06/1916
War Diary	Lederzeele	19/06/1916	19/06/1916
War Diary	Leulinghem	20/06/1916	30/06/1916
Heading	3rd Divisional Engineers 1/1st Cheshire Field Company R.E. July 1916		
War Diary	St Omer Area	01/07/1916	31/07/1916
Heading	3rd Divisional Engineers 1/1st Cheshire Field Company R.E. August 1916		
War Diary		01/08/1916	31/08/1916
Heading	3rd Divisional Engineers 1/1st Cheshire Field Company R.E. September 1916		
War Diary		01/09/1916	30/09/1916
War Diary			
Heading	3rd Divisional Engineers 1/1st Cheshire Field Company R.E. October 1916		
War Diary		01/10/1916	31/10/1916
Miscellaneous	1/1 Cheshire Field Coy Order		
Heading	3rd Divisional Engineers 1/1st Cheshire Field Company R.E. November 1916		
War Diary		01/11/1916	17/11/1916
Heading	3rd Divisional Engineers 1/1st Cheshire Field Company R.E. December 1916		
War Diary		01/12/1916	31/12/1916
Miscellaneous	Casualties		
Heading	3rd Division War Diaries 438th Cheshire Field Coy January To 31st December 1917		
War Diary		01/01/1917	23/06/1917

War Diary	Lebucquiere	01/07/1917	30/11/1917
Miscellaneous	Casualties		
War Diary		01/12/1917	31/12/1917
Heading	3rd Division War Diaries 438th Cheshire Field Coy 1918 Jan-1919 Oct		
War Diary		01/01/1918	28/02/1918
War Diary	Casualties		
Heading	3rd Divisional Engineers 438th (Cheshire) Field Company R.E. March 1918		
Heading	War Diary 438th (Cheshire) Fd. Co. R.E. Month Of March 1918		
War Diary		01/03/1918	31/03/1918
Heading	3rd Divisional Engineers War Diary 438th (Cheshire) Field Company R.E. April 1918		
War Diary		01/04/1918	30/04/1918
Miscellaneous	438 Field Coy.		
War Diary	Forward Billets Vendin Rear Billets Reveilon Wood	01/05/1918	08/05/1918
War Diary	Rear Billets Reveilon Wood	09/05/1918	18/05/1918
War Diary	Reveillon Wood	19/05/1918	31/05/1918
War Diary	HQ. At Bois De Reveillon	01/06/1918	30/06/1918
War Diary	Work In Locon Sector	01/06/1918	30/06/1918
War Diary	HQ At Bois De Reveillon	19/06/1918	19/06/1918
War Diary	Work In Locon Sector	20/06/1918	30/06/1918
War Diary	H Q At Bois De Reveillon	01/07/1918	31/07/1918
War Diary	Work In Locon Sector	01/07/1918	31/07/1918
War Diary		09/07/1918	20/07/1918
War Diary		01/07/1918	22/07/1918
War Diary	H Q At Bois De Reveillon	23/07/1918	25/07/1918
War Diary	Work In Locon Sector	26/07/1918	31/07/1918
War Diary	H Q At Bois De Reveillon	01/08/1918	07/08/1918
War Diary	Work In Locon Sector	01/08/1918	07/08/1918
War Diary		01/08/1918	21/12/1918
War Diary	Duren	22/12/1918	31/12/1918
War Diary	Duren Germany	01/01/1919	01/03/1919
War Diary	Duren	02/03/1919	02/03/1919
War Diary	Kerpen	03/03/1919	03/03/1919
War Diary	Cologne (Braunsfeld)	04/03/1919	16/03/1919
War Diary	Cologne (Braunsfeld)	17/03/1919	31/03/1919
War Diary	Germany Cologne		
War Diary	Germany Cologne (Braunsfeld)	01/04/1919	05/09/1919
War Diary	Riehl	06/09/1919	30/09/1919
War Diary	Riehl Cologne	01/05/1919	30/10/1919

WD 95
(403/3
5b9a

2nd Division
War Diaries
1/1st Cheshire Field Coy R.E.

~~Dec 1914~~
~~Jany.~~ To December
1916

Re numbered 438

Index	SUBJECT.	3RD DIV
No.	Contents.	Date.

R.E.
CHESHIRE FIELD COY.

WAR DIARY.
~~JAN-DEC~~ 1915

1914 DEC - 1915 DEC

1/1 Cheshires
F Coy

WAR DIARY
INTELLIGENCE SUMMARY.
(Erase heading not required.)

Army Form C. 2118.

Hour, Date, Place	Summary of Events and Information	Remarks and references to Appendices
Dec. 1914		
1st to 7th	At Northampton preparing for service overseas	
8th	Entrained for Southampton. On arrival proceeded to rest camp. Capt. MacLean left at Northampton sick	
9th	Embarked "Glenavon Head"	
10th	Landed at Havre. proceeded to Rest Camp No 1.	
13th	Entrained for St Omer	
14th	Detrained & marched to billets at "Renescure"	
16th	Capt. MacLean rejoined	
20th	Received orders to attack on the morrow at Croix de Poperinghe via Hazebrouck & Bailleul	
21st	Marched in Column of Route to Hazebrouck & billeted there for night	
22nd	Left Hazebrouck & arrived destination 3pm. Here the Coy was split up on Section width 56" Corps on No 57" = two with H.Q. to the Cond. of Coy	
23rd	No 1 Section with 57 Corps went to Kemmel	
24th	for duty on the Trenches & supporting points	

Army Form C. 2118.

WAR DIARY
or
INTELLIGENCE SUMMARY.
(Erase heading not required.)

Instructions regarding War Diaries and Intelligence Summaries are contained in F.S. Regs., Part II. and the Staff Manual respectively. Title pages will be prepared in manuscript.

Hour, Date, Place	Summary of Events and Information	Remarks and references to Appendices
25*	From Army	
27*	No 3 & 4 Section with Corps Cy Reinot ST. at Kemmel	
31*	No 2 with 5 y. O.R.E. relieve Corps Cy	
	During the periods when the various Coys were not at Kemmel they were employed repairing Roads, hutting & trenching Kopp) Proven in Rivetting Breastwork mg & wire entanglements	

ARMY TROOPS

Archie Field Coy: R.E. (T)

1-1-15

Vol I 1.12.14 — 28.2.15

Army Form C. 2118.

WAR DIARY
or
INTELLIGENCE SUMMARY.
(Erase heading not required.)

Instructions regarding War Diaries and Intelligence Summaries are contained in F.S. Regs., Part II. and the Staff Manual respectively. Title pages will be prepared in manuscript.

Hour, Date, Place	Summary of Events and Information	Remarks and references to Appendices
Jany 1st 1915 LA CLYTTE	No 2 section with 57th Score at KEMMEL worked on Trench & supporting from. Recruiting training in Nos 1, 3, +4. Road repairing	
2"	— do —	
3"	— do —	
4"	No 1 section with 56th Co RE & KEMMEL worked on Trench & supporting fires	
	Nos 2, 3, +4 Road repairing	
5"	— do —	
6"	— do —	
7"	— do —	
8" 9" 10" 11"	No 3 +4 with Compo Co to LA CLYTTE worked on Trenches & recent line	
	No 1 at KEMMEL worked as before. No 1 Road repairing	
12"	No 1 joined Compo Co at LA CLYTTE No 1, 3, 4 worked on & type dkts	
	line. No 2 at KEMMEL worked as before	
13" 14" 15"	— do — — do — — do —	
16"	No 2 joined up with 1, 3, 4, + Cheshire Field CoyRE were on	
	new work	
17" to 31st	Work of various kinds were carried on in the Trenches & Supports line K L & M sections by sections alternately. The sections	
	remaining at LA CLYTTE worked on the building of this	
	Laundry Bath house Drainage of field + cleaning of	
	billets.	

McKergow Major
Cheshire Field CoyRE

Forms/C. 2118/20

Army Form C. 2118.

WAR DIARY
or
INTELLIGENCE SUMMARY.
(Erase heading not required.)

Instructions regarding War Diaries and Intelligence Summaries are contained in F. S. Regs., Part II. and the Staff Manual respectively. Title pages will be prepared in manuscript.

Hour, Date, Place	Summary of Events and Information	Remarks and references to Appendices
1st Feb. 1915 @ La Clytte.	Nos 1 & 2 sections at Vierstraat working on trenches. Remainder Company building huts at Acre and stables & Lean-tos for Brigade at La Clytte	2 sections always at forward billet working on trenches as required day and night
2nd " "	Nos 1 & 2 sections at Vierstraat working on sections trenches & collecting materials for entanglements. Remainder collecting & transporting timber to 42 huts at La Clytte.	
3rd " "	Commenced O.C. Stables hut @ Schoenberg. Continued stabling.	
	300 1 Section returned to La Clytte. No 4 @ Vierstraat working on trenches. Remainder completed hut @ Schoenberg. Sorting out timber making frames. Laying out & erecting sites for La Clytte huts.	
4th " "	No 3 Section goes Vierstraat. Remainder La Clytte huts	
5th " "	Continued huts	
6th " "		
7th " "	No 3 returns from Vierstraat. No 2 arrives to new forward billet Lindenhoek farm. Remainder continues huts & collecting timber from Bailleul. Shopping from Reninghelst.	
8th " "	Continued huts & collecting timber & top poles	
9th " "	— do — No 2 returns No 4 proceeds Vierstraat	
10th " "	— do —	
11th " "	— do — No 3 proceeds No 1 returns. Commenced commandants completed hut-at Schoenberg to replace one burnt.	
12th " "	Continued huts & collected timber. Also built coal depot to Brigade.	
13th " "	— do — shopholes. No 2 proceeds No 4 returns Vierstraat	
14th " "	Continued huts with assistance by "C" Section also Infantry Carpenters & working party { No 1 proceeds No 3 returns Vierstraat }	
15th " "	— do — No 4 " No 2 " "	
16th " "	— do —	
17th " "	— do —	
18th " "	— do —	
19th " "	{ Also waterproofing huts with & Schoenberg } { No 3 proceeds No 1 returns }	
20th " "	Completed 42 huts & Commenced 4 additional No 2 " No 4 "	
21st " "	Continued 4 huts	
22nd " "	— " — Completed some. Commenced mess hut No 1 proceeds No 3 returns "	
23rd " "		

Army Form C. 2118.

WAR DIARY
or
INTELLIGENCE SUMMARY.
(Erase heading not required.)

Instructions regarding War Diaries and Intelligence Summaries are contained in F. S. Regs., Part II. and the Staff Manual respectively. Title pages will be prepared in manuscript.

Hour, Date, Place	Summary of Events and Information	Remarks and references to Appendices
24th Feb. 1915 @ La Clytte	Continued map that. weather broken, hut me @ Schonpenberg + bicycle shed at Brigade H Q.	
25th " "	Continued as above also dug trench for grenade throwing practice	
26th " "	" " No 2 practice grenade throwing. No 4 proceed to Zootium Barracks	Aircraft at 17 base details arrived. Sergt. Mathis wounded in Thigh about 11 p.m. 26/2/15
27th " "	Commenced replacing straw huts @ Schonpenberg with wooden ones (No 3 proceed to Zootium Barracks)	
28th " "	Continued Schonpenberg huts	

Wilson Major
Chatham Pier Coy E

121/1940.

ATK

3rd Division

Cheshire Field Coy. R.E.

Vol II   1 – 31.3.15.

WAR DIARY or INTELLIGENCE SUMMARY

Army Form C. 2118.

Instructions regarding War Diaries and Intelligence Summaries are contained in F.S. Regs., Part II. and the Staff Manual respectively. Title pages will be prepared in manuscript.

(Erase heading not required.)

Hour, Date, Place	Summary of Events and Information	Remarks and references to Appendices
1st March 1915 — LA CLYTTE	No 2 proceeds to Vrouwedyk farm to work on trenches. Remainder build bridge. No 4 returns from Scherpenberg. (at La Clytte hut)	Sections at VROUWEDYK farm working on trenches as required day & night.
2nd — do —	Continued construction huts at Scherpenberg.	
3rd — do —	— do —	
4th — do —	— do —	No 1 proceeds No 3 returns Vrouwedyk	
5th — do —	— do —	No 3 experimenting with ammonal	
6th — do —	— do —	Ave Guan stable @ LA CLYTTE. No 2 returns. No 4 proceeds to VROUWEDYK	
7th — do —	— do —	No 2 cleaning up in stables. Cattle picketed	
8th — do —	— do —	{No 2 experimenting with ammonal	
		No 1 returns. No 3 goes to VROUWEDYK	
9th — do —	— do —		
10th — do —	— do —	{No 2 carried on with ammonal experiments	
		No 4 returns. No 2 goes to VROUWEDYK	
		No 4 experiments with carpeting	
11th — do —	— do —	— do — No 3 returns. No 1 goes to VROUWEDYK	
12th — do —	{Remainder collected top poles for own stables & building Jam	
	also complete bridge into football field for RAMC @ LA CLYTTE	
13th — do —	{Remainder picked own stables – Commenced forge hut @ VROUWEDYK	
	No 2 returns. No 4 proceeds to VROUWEDYK	
	also complete stables & carried on with snow hut @ LOCRE	
14th — do —	— do —	Carried on with snow hut @ LOCRE. No 1 returns. No 3 goes VROUWEDYK	
15th — do —	Completed Forge + Scherpenberg huts. Collected timber from CAILLEUL to Laundry @ LA CLYTTE	
16th — do —	Commenced Laundry @ LA CLYTTE. No 2 proceeds to No 4 returns from VROUWEDYK	
17th — do —	Carried on with Laundry. Collected stones for No 4 squad ditch	
18th — do —	— do — No 1 proceeds to VROUWEDYK	
19th — do —	— do — No 4 — do —	
20th — do —	— do — No 3 returns from — do —	
21st — do —	— do — Repaired bridge at RAMC wagon path. Remainder knife rests	
22nd — do —	— do — {Commenced RE shoe @ LA CLYTTE. Paths and internal fences	
	in m/stone rubo nest. Path waterproofing. Huts roofs at SCHERPENBERG	
	waterproofing material to RE Park at DICKEBUSCH	
23rd — do —	— do — {Carrying parties with trench nets. Loopholes. No 2 returns from VROUWEDYK	
24th — do —	— do — transporting materials to DICKEBUSCH	

Army Form C. 2118.

WAR DIARY
or
INTELLIGENCE SUMMARY.
(Erase heading not required.)

Instructions regarding War Diaries and Intelligence Summaries are contained in F. S. Regs., Part II. and the Staff Manual respectively. Title pages will be prepared in manuscript.

Hour, Date, Place	Summary of Events and Information	Remarks and references to Appendices
LA CLYTTE 25th March 1915	Carpenters working on Lamneys at LA CLYTTE. Reman on knife rests, petrol oil carts, loopholes. No 3 proceeds to & return from VROUWEDYK. Working on knife rests etc	
26th ---	Working on knife rests etc	
27th ---	—do—	
28th ---	No 4 returns. No 2 proceeds to VROUWEDYK	
29th ---	Collecting material & excavating bus to G.2 trenches & Rifle House	
30th ---	No 3 returns to & proceeds VROUWEDYK	
31st ---	Collecting materials. Commences carrying gas bar.	

A.W. Harper Major

121/5254

3rd Division

Archie Field Coy RE

Vol III 1 - 30.4.15

WAR DIARY
or
INTELLIGENCE SUMMARY.
(Erase heading not required.)

Army Form C. 2118.

Instructions regarding War Diaries and Intelligence Summaries are contained in F.S. Regs., Part II. and the Staff Manual respectively. Title pages will be prepared in manuscript.

Hour, Date, Place	Summary of Events and Information	Remarks and references to Appendices
1 April 1915 LA CLYTTE	No 2 Section returns from front billet at VROWEDYK FARM. Work to No 4. previous to	
2 " "	Towards hut to keep gun completed	
3 " "	Worked in ROWEDYK continued making wire entanglement &	
4 " "	SM13 proceeded [ ] front billet " " "	
5 " "	No 1 returned [ ] front billet " " "	
6 " "	Section at LA CLYTTE worked on Pioneer Shops & various jobs	
7 " "	No 2 Section to VROWEDYK. No 4 Section proceed 56" CORE at DICKEBUSCH	
8 " "	Section in front billet still on job. [ ] work to Rotoman & Care Sect	
9 " "	No 1 Section returned from front billet. No 1 proceeded. Work in Pioneer Shops	
10 " "	Work & odd jobs in Pioneer Shops continued	
11 " "	[ ] through & dam commenced at LA CLYTTE Huts	
12 " "	No 3 Section to front billet No 2 + 3. No 1 return. Continue Water Supply	
13 " "	continued in water Supply at & Rue Jones to Lain sick	
14 " "	1/2 No 1 to front billet " " " " " "	
15 " "	Various odd jobs in Pioneer Shops " " "	
16 " "	No 3 + 2 No 1 Return. No 2 proceed to from from billet	
17 " "	Commenced taking down Huts at WESTOUTRE	
18 " "	Commenced erecting huts at ROSEN HILL	
19 " "	Continued " " " "	Put down W^m McWilliam L/Cpl to water
20 " "	" " " "	
21 " "	" " " "	Capt S Cunningham accounted sick Hut for
22 " "	" " " "	
23 " "	9" [ ] Gun Battery Section Canadian Capt'n employed	
24 " "	No 3 Sect to No 1 Road VROWEDYK No 3+ No 1 return Capt AT MacLea apodean	
25 " "	Capt MacIver died from Wounds at LA CLYTTE Bridge but sent to YPRES. Huts at ROSEN HILL continued L+ B A DUNCAN + 30 O R arrived	

Army Form C. 2118.

WAR DIARY
INTELLIGENCE SUMMARY.
(Erase heading not required.)

Instructions regarding War Diaries and Intelligence Summaries are contained in F. S. Regs., Part II. and the Staff Manual respectively. Title pages will be prepared in manuscript.

Hour, Date, Place	Summary of Events and Information	Remarks and references to Appendices
26 April 1915 LA CLYTTE	Units at ROSENHILL continued & RAM & HdQrs at LA CLYTTE	
27 " " "	" " " " "	
28 " " "	" " " " "	
29 " " "	" " " " "	
30 " " "	" " " " "	

121/5775.

3rd Division.

Arthur Field Coy: R.E.

Vol IV 1 — 31.5.15.

WAR DIARY

INTELLIGENCE SUMMARY

Army Form C. 2118.

Instructions regarding War Diaries and Intelligence Summaries are contained in F.S. Regs., Part II. and the Staff Manual respectively. Title pages will be prepared in manuscript.

(Erase heading not required.)

Hour, Date, Place	Summary of Events and Information	Remarks and references to Appendices
1st May 1915	No 1 & No 2 Sections went to forward billet for 4 days work in firing line	Sections at forward billet worked on firing line, communication trenches &c as required
2nd "	No. 3 & 4 Sect - Making horse troughs - Roofing of Medical Hut - Repairing floor of various huts in use by the Brigade	
3rd "	Commenced Building Dam, Reservoir & Filter at LOCYTTE. All available men went at night to put up wire entanglements near VOORMEZEELE.	
4th "	Work continued on Dam & Reservoir, & erecting improvised huts with tarpaulins	
5th "	" No 3 & No 4 proceed to } forward billet.	
6th "	" No 1 & No 2 return from }	
7th "	" 2nd Lt. A.I. Eastwood joined unit.	
8th "	" + collecting hop-poles	
9th "	" + erecting hut for Sanitary Section. All available men, drivers included went to VOORMEZEELE to put farm in state of defence.	
10th "	{ No 1 & No 2 proceed to } forward billet. Lt. Krikk wounded.	
"	{ No 3 & No 4 return from } Work continued on Dam & Reservoir and also at BOORMEZEELE. Lt. Eastwood wounded.	
12th "	" ...	
13th "	" ... 2/Lt. C.A.S. Ft. Moore joined for duty.	
14th "	{No 1 & No 3 proceed to } forward billet. Party continued work on Reservoir + building dugouts at Vierstraat	
15th "	{No 1 & No 2 return from } No 2 & No 1 proceeded to } forward No 3 R.E. returned from } billet	
16th May	" + dugouts at Vierstraat.	
17th "	" ...	
18th "	" + dugouts at Vierstraat.	
20th "	" ...	
21st "	" ...	
22nd/24th "	" ...	
25th "	" last that proceed to forward billet. Section (Hay) with 56th C.R.E. returned	
26th "	Sections recalled from forward billet - returned to wanted to ready to rejoin us. Work continued on Reservoir	

Army Form C. 2118.

WAR DIARY
INTELLIGENCE SUMMARY.
(Erase heading not required.)

Instructions regarding War Diaries and Intelligence Summaries are contained in F. S. Regs., Part II. and the Staff Manual respectively. Title pages will be prepared in manuscript.

Hour, Date, Place	Summary of Events and Information	Remarks and references to Appendices
27th May 1915. La Clytte & Ypres	3rd Divn ordered to proceed to take up part of the line in Ypres Salient. Company paraded at 2.30 p.m. marched to rendezvous behind Ypres where No.1 Section joined us. In the evening Officers & NCOs went out to reconnoitre the new line. Company proceeded to billets (upsides) to Ploegsteert, most of the horses when sent back to behind Vlamertinghe	
28th to 31st May 1915. Ypres.	All men worked at night in firing line building new trenches, wiring, digging communication trenches to.	

L. A. Hallowes
Lt
Actg. O.C. Cheshire Field Co. R.E.

131/6063

3rd Division

Archie Field Coy: RE.

Vol I 1 — 30.6.15.

Army Form C.2118.

WAR DIARY
or
INTELLIGENCE SUMMARY.
(Erase heading not required.)

Instructions regarding War Diaries and Intelligence Summaries are contained in F.S. Regs., Part II. and the Staff Manual respectively. Title pages will be prepared in manuscript.

Hour, Date, Place	Summary of Events and Information	Remarks and references to Appendices
1915.		
June 1/2.	Two Sections worked on Communication trenches in daytime & 2 Sections at night wiring in front line.	
June 3	Party sent to repair Pontoon Bridge. 2 Sections on C.T.s during day & two at night wiring in front line.	
June 4/5/6	Two Sections on C.T.s in daytime & two at night wiring in front line.	
June 7	" " " " " " " Two Sections today building heads dug outs. At night three (two) sections were wiring in front line.	
June 8th	7th Lt. A. Halsall & Lt. G. A. Duncan both slightly wounded. Lt Halsall returned to duty & Lt Duncan evacuated to base hospital. Two sections worked by day on C.T.s & two at night sandbagging in front line.	
June 9/12	" " " " " + two at night revetting, wiring etc. in front line marking out assembly trenches in preparation for 16th	
June 13	One Section worked by day on new dugouts. 3 Sections at night on new C.T. from [trench] 65 to [trench] 63	
June 14	" " " " " " to day " " " . All sections worked at night	
June 15	marking out assembly trenches & cutting gaps in hedges. 1 NCO killed, 5 wounded. Day was spent preparing for attack on 16th. A guard of 1 NCO 16 men which was on the Pontoon bridge was relieved by 76 F.C. in the town returning through two a shell burst in the square & wounded 5 of the sappers. NCO & 1 sapper suffering from shock. Coy. left billets at 8 pm to take their place in the line & moved into assembly trenches. No.1 Section was attached to 1st Lincolns. No.3 to 2nd Scottish. Nos 2+4 to Royal Irish Rifles for the purpose of digging a C.T. from our present front. to the captured trenches.	
June 16	At 2.50 am our bombardment began. At 4.15 am the attacking troops advanced took the first line trenches. The supporting troops advanced with them & 3 Sections were to keep to consolidate the captured position as quickly as possible. The attack had meanwhile progressed to the German 2nd line & places as far as the 3rd line. No.2+4 Sections were told by CO. R.I.R. to standby and await orders. A digging party of 150 which was at our

WAR DIARY
INTELLIGENCE SUMMARY

Army Form C. 2118.

Hour, Date, Place	Summary of Events and Information	Remarks and references to Appendices
1915		
June 16 contd.	disposal had advanced with the attack. The situation appeared uncertain on our left, and it was not until 2 P.m. that the officers of 2nd Section were sent for with ref. to the C.T. An officer went to reconnoitre the ground & found that the sunken road leading forwards from our old line to the captured 1st line was clear from view & rifle fire to anyone going up. At 3 P.m. a minor amount of the left was don't-inspected, the question of the C.T. was therefore left in abeyance as the sunken Rd. afforded good communication. Later, finding that the two sections were unable to carry on with the C.T. until orders were received, they were employed in collecting all materials & stores which could be found & forming them into one depôt. 1 & 3 Sections were still with the battn. to which they had been attached, consolidating the position. At dusk the company was relieved by 56th Co. & returned to billets. Total casualties for the day – 6 N.C.Os & 17 Sappers wounded. 2 Sappers killed. 1 N.C.O. & 1 Sapper missing.	
June 17th	Carpenters resting.	
June 18th	All available men at night works on-headquarters in front line	
June 19	Coy. worked 2 daily hrs dug outs. Major Kenyon proceeded to England on duty. Command handed over to R.W. & Aokan.	
June 20	Coy. worked on New dug outs.	
June 21	Two sections worked on a supporting point & two on the dug outs. The two sections working on the supporting point were relieved about 18hrs. as the whole Co. was wanted for work at night on the firing line at F0090.	
June 22	Coy. worked 1 day on the New dug outs.	

Army Form C. 2118.

WAR DIARY
—or—
INTELLIGENCE SUMMARY.
(Erase heading not required.)

Instructions regarding War Diaries and Intelligence Summaries are contained in F. S. Regs., Part II. and the Staff Manual respectively. Title pages will be prepared in manuscript.

Hour, Date, Place	Summary of Events and Information	Remarks and references to Appendices
June 23rd	Two sections worked on Supporting Point & two on the new dug out B.	
June 24th	Work - same as for 23rd. Sapper Jarvis tried by F.G. Court Martial for threatening a superior officer. Found guilty & sentenced to 84 days F.P. President No.1.	
June 25/26	Two sections worked on the Supporting Point and two sections back in billets were taken in musketry & Company transport.	
June 27th	Work & training — same as for 25/26th. Church Service 5 P.M.	
June 28	Work & training - As for 27th. Lt. R. C. Duncan returned to duty from Hospital. 2nd Lt. C. P. Watson joined unit from England.	
June 29/30	Two sections worked on the redoubt. The two sections in billets had company drill, rifle exercise, musketry etc.	

M Halsall Lt.
1/OC Cheshire Field Co. R.E.

3rd /5 Division

121/6357

Cheshire Field Coy RE
No VIII
July 15

Army Form C. 2118

WAR DIARY
or
INTELLIGENCE SUMMARY.
(Erase heading not required.)

Instructions regarding War Diaries and Intelligence Summaries are contained in F. S. Regs., Part II. and the Staff Manual respectively. Title pages will be prepared in manuscript.

Hour, Date, Place	Summary of Events and Information	Remarks and references to Appendices
July 1915.		
1st & 2nd	Two sections worked on supporting point nr Zillebeke. Two resting Sections — infantry training, musketry &c.	
3rd & 4th	Work — same as for 1st & 2nd except that party of men from resting section commenced making trench horses.	
5th	Two sections worked on Supporting point and from today will stay in SANCTUARY WOOD in dug outs for 3 days. The two other three days resting sections relieve them in then. Resting Sections — Company drill, musketry &c. and making trench boards.	
6th & 7th	Work — same as for 5th. Evening of 7th Sections relieves in Sanctuary Wood.	
8th	Of the two forward Sections, one worked on Supporting point and one making dressing station & splinter proofs for wounded in SANCTUARY WOOD. Two resting sections was party of 6 on trench boards, parades in evening to repair roads nr Zillebeke.	
9th & 10th	Ditto	
11th & 12th	Sections relieved in Sanctuary Wood. All available men of resting sections repairing roads near OUDERDOM.	
13th & 14th	Work for two forward sections the same viz. Supporting point & splinter proofs in wood. Party (g resting Section) marches out near to Ypres, Enfranced the infantry (q digging party in the evening. All remaining men sent to collect heavy material from Ypres.	
15th	Two sections ceased fm today to live in Sanctuary Wood, that schedule the splinter proofs being finished. Parties as yesterday.	
16th	Two sections commenced work on new schedule. One section was shelled off the work soon after they started. So returned to billets until dusk & went after dark to continue. Parties as usual.	

(9 29 6) W 4141—463 100,000 9/14 H W V Forms/C. 2118/10

Army Form C. 2118.

WAR DIARY
— or —
INTELLIGENCE SUMMARY.
(Erase heading not required.)

(2)

Instructions regarding War Diaries and Intelligence Summaries are contained in F.S. Regs., Part II. and the Staff Manual respectively. Title pages will be prepared in manuscript.

Hour, Date, Place	Summary of Events and Information	Remarks and references to Appendices
July 1915 18th / 19th	One Section worked on redoubt by day & one section on other redoubt by night. Parties building a roadtrestle, Hub, Handbars to avoid.	
20th – 21st		
22nd	One section on redoubt. Parties on Kostrecole Hubye, & preparing charges for demolition of bridge. 8.0 p.m. All available train sent on road repairing.	
23rd	Coy. moved to new billet near Dickebush	
24th to 26th	All available Carpenters from Two resting Sections working on new Hub for III Div H.Q. Remainder unloading wagons releasing up billets. Fatigue party collecting bricks from Ypres.	
27th	Two sections commenced work in new sector of firing line. Party sent to build dug out near Brigade H.Q. Parties as usual on III Div Hut, collecting bricks re. from Ypres.	
28th to 31st	Ditto.	

Maisley Lt
for O.C. Cheshire Field Coy.

121/6598

3rd Division

11 Arthur Field Coy RE

Vol VII

From 1 - 31. 8. 15

WAR DIARY or INTELLIGENCE SUMMARY.

Army Form C. 2118

Hour, Date, Place	Summary of Events and Information	Remarks and references to Appendices
Aug 1st 1915	Two sections (Nos 2 & 4) were working in FIRING LINE in the wood J.34, improving traverses and drains &c. All carpenters from Sections 1 & 3 were working on huts at RENINGHELST for III Divn Headquarters. Remainder were constructing shelters & review for billets.	
Aug 2nd	Ditto	
Aug 3rd	"	
Aug 4th	Sections 2 & 4 in FIRING LINE. Capt Flint to Hospital. Sections 1 & 3 working in FIRING LINE, made new dugout in wood J.34, and were constructing landing place for flying boat bridge over Yser canal at Trench No 28. Carpenters working at RENINGHELS on huts for III Divn Headquarters. material was collected from Ypres for defensible works.	
Aug 5th	As for 4th, except that section in the FIRING LINE started making a new machine gun emplacement at LOCK POST.	
Aug 6th	Sections in FIRING LINE marked out communication trench from Trench No 39 to CANAL BANK. Work was also commenced on driving forward No 1A gallery and making emplacements in Nos 2 & 3 galleries in the BLUFF. Resting sections as per 4th inst.	

Army Form C. 2118.

WAR DIARY
or
INTELLIGENCE SUMMARY.
(Erase heading not required.)

Instructions regarding War Diaries and Intelligence Summaries are contained in F. S. Regs., Part II. and the Staff Manual respectively. Title pages will be prepared in manuscript.

Hour, Date, Place	Summary of Events and Information	Remarks and references to Appendices
Aug 1915 Sheet N⁰ 2. Aug 4th & 8th	Sections working in FIRING LINE worked on driving N⁰ 1A Gallery in the BLUFF and completed the emplacement in N⁰ 2 gallery. Work was also carried on in N⁰ 3 gallery in the BLUFF and the machine gun emplacement at LOCK POST. Carpenters of resting sections were working on huts for III Div. Headquarters at RENINGHELS. Parties in Ypres obtaining material for defence work, but were turned back on 8th inst. Capt Flint invalided to ENGLAND on the 8th inst.	[signature]
Aug 9th	Sections in FIRING LINE carried on with work as above, but in addition assisted motor machine gun Section working on machine gun emplacements in the GORDON POST. Resting Sections carried on with work as above, but three working at huts and the (word) Section did musketry drill.	[signature]
Aug 10th	N⁰s 2 & 4 Sections proceeded to forward billets in wood I 34, and Sections 1 & 3 returned to back billet. Sections 2 & 4 carried on with work in galleries in the BLUFF, and machine gun emplacement in LOCK POST. Carpenters still working at RENINGHELS on huts for III Div. Head quarters.	[signature]

Army Form C. 2118.

WAR DIARY
or
INTELLIGENCE SUMMARY.
(Erase heading not required.)

Instructions regarding War Diaries and Intelligence Summaries are contained in F.S. Regs., Part II. and the Staff Manual respectively. Title pages will be prepared in manuscript.

Hour, Date, Place	Summary of Events and Information	Remarks and references to Appendices
Aug 1915 Sheet N°3. Aug 11th	Sections Nos 2 + 4 in the FIRING LINE carried on w/t driving N°1A gallery in the BLUFF, and making machine gun emplacement in LOCKPOST, also assisted heavy machine gun Section working on machine gun emplacement in the GORDON POST. The Carpenters were still working on huts for III Div Headquarters at RENINGHELS. The party working Sections were preparing material for VIII & IX Field Ambulances. A party went to DICKEBUSCH to obtain eight railway material from DICKEBUSCH LAKE.	[signature]
Aug 12th to 13th to 14th	The Sections in the FIRING LINE carried on as above. The Carpenters were still working at RENINGHELS on huts for III Div Headquarters. Material was being prepared for VIII & IX Field Ambulance. Roof of hut for VIII IX Field Ambulance was repaired. Communication trench for supporting point at BEDFORD HOUSE was worked out for infantry working party.	[signature]

WAR DIARY
or
INTELLIGENCE SUMMARY.
(Erase heading not required.)

Army Form C. 2118.

Instructions regarding War Diaries and Intelligence Summaries are contained in F.S. Regs., Part II. and the Staff Manual respectively. Title pages will be prepared in manuscript.

Hour, Date, Place	Summary of Events and Information	Remarks and references to Appendices
Aug 1915. Sheet No. 4. II. Aug 15th to 16th	Sections Nos 2 & 4 working in the FIRING LINE carried on with driving No 1A gallery in the BLUFF, and also worked on machine gun emplacements in the GORDON POST, on top of the BLUFF and at LOCKPOST. The resting Sections carried on preparing material for the VIII & IX Field Ambulance. No mid Section and resting Section had company drill. Church service was held. Carpenters were still employed at REWING HELS on huts for the III Divn Headquarters.	[signature]
Aug 14th	Section Nos 1 to 3 relieved Sections Nos 2 & 4 in the FIRING LINE, and carried on with driving No 1A gallery in the BLUFF, and making dug-outs in galleries Nos 2 & 3 Resting Sections carried on with preparing material for the VIII & IX th Field Ambulance, and fitting windows to hut of the IX th Field Ambulance and making a new culvert at entrance.	[signature]
Aug 18th to 19th	Ditto	[signature]

Army Form C. 2118.

WAR DIARY
or
INTELLIGENCE SUMMARY.
(Erase heading not required.)

Instructions regarding War Diaries and Intelligence Summaries are contained in F.S. Regs., Part II. and the Staff Manual respectively. Title pages will be prepared in manuscript.

Hour, Date, Place	Summary of Events and Information	Remarks and references to Appendices
Aug 19, 1915 (Shell N.9) Aug 20th	Sections Nos 1 & 3 were relieved in FIRING LINE by 2/1 North Midland Field Co. R.E. The preparation of Material for VIIth & IXth Field Ambulances were carried on.	[signature]
Aug 21st	Company drill for whole Company. Taking over new line with 9th Brigade.	[signature]
Aug 22nd	Work was commenced on communication trench in South Bank of ZILLEBEKE LAKE, and to improve and north of communication trench between ZILLEBEKE and MAPLE COPSE	[signature]
Aug 23rd & 24th	As for 22nd. Ablution trenches, latrines were erected at HOOGRAF for VIIIth Field Ambulance.	[signature]
Aug 25th, 26th, 27th, 28th, 29th	By night superior were given to infantry working parties on ZILLEBEKE & MAPLE COPSE communication trench, and by day parties from the unit worked on roofing and laying of track roads.	[signature]

Army Form C. 2118.

WAR DIARY
or
~~INTELLIGENCE SUMMARY.~~
(Erase heading not required.)

Instructions regarding War Diaries and Intelligence Summaries are contained in F. S. Regs., Part II. and the Staff Manual respectively. Title pages will be prepared in manuscript.

Hour, Date, Place	Summary of Events and Information	Remarks and references to Appendices
Aug 1915 (Sheet No 6) Aug 30 to 31st	Work on the communication trench between ZILLEBEKE and MAPLE COPSE was carried on by infantry working parties at night and working parties from this unit by day. Work was carried out by infantry working parties under the supervision of Officers, N.C.Os and men of this unit. On the supporting point near the MOATED GRANGE Lieut Challoner joined unit on 31st from Glasgow. (Fortress) R.E.	[signature] J Wayte [?] Capt. O.C. 1st Ches Fd. Coy. R.E.

3rd Kinross

121/7082

1/1 Lothian Field Co. RE.

Pte W111

Sep 1. 15

Army Form C. 2118.

WAR DIARY
or
INTELLIGENCE SUMMARY.
(Erase heading not required.)

Instructions regarding War Diaries and Intelligence Summaries are contained in F.S. Regs., Part II. and the Staff Manual respectively. Title pages will be prepared in manuscript.

Hour, Date, Place	Summary of Events and Information	Remarks and references to Appendices
Sept 1915 The Field.		
Sept 1st, 2nd & 3rd	By night parties from this unit supervised the infantry working parties on the communication trench in the South Bank of ZILLEBEKE LAKE and also in DORMY HOUSE LANE. A party also supervised the infantry working on the two supporting points near the MOATED GRANGE. By day a party from this unit worked on revetting and laying trench boards in DORMY HOUSE LANE, and assistance was also given to the artillery making dug outs at ECLUSE No 9.	J Waynehouse Capt RE(T)
Sept 4th	Work was carried on as above By night a party from this unit worked out the line of a new Communication trench between MAPLE COPSE and the junction of OXFORD and REGENT STREETS A party was detailed on making trench boards & trellis.	J Waynehouse Capt RE(T)
Sept 5th, 6th, and 7th	By night parties from this unit supervised the infantry parties working on the communication trenches in the South Bank of ZILLEBEKE LAKE, DORMY HOUSE LANE, and OXFORD STREETS and supporting points near the MOATED GRANGE. and supporting points near MOATED GRANGE. A party from this unit repaired the ZILLEBEKE ROAD at I.22.c.5.d By day a party worked on revetting and laying trench boards in DORMY HOUSE LANE	J Waynehouse Capt RE(T)
Sept 8th, 9th, 10th	By night parties supervised the infantry parties on the communication trenches and supporting points mentioned above. By day work was carried on in DORMY HOUSE LANE	J Waynehouse Capt RE(T)

Army Form C. 2118.

WAR DIARY
or
INTELLIGENCE SUMMARY.
(Erase heading not required.)

Instructions regarding War Diaries and Intelligence Summaries are contained in F.S. Regs., Part II. and the Staff Manual respectively. Title pages will be prepared in manuscript.

Hour, Date, Place	Summary of Events and Information	Remarks and references to Appendices
Sept 11th & Sept 1915.	By night parties from this unit supervised infantry working parties on the communication trench between MAPLE COPSE and its junction of OXFORD and REGENT STREETS, and the DORMY HOUSE LANE, also the party	
Sept 11th, 12th	route via MOATED GRANGE. By day a party supervised the infantry party working on the communication trench in the South Bank of ZILLEBEKE LAKE. A day party also worked on revetting & laying trench boards in DORMY HOUSE LANE.	J.W.Reynoldson
Sept 13th	By night a party supervised the infantry working party in DORMY HOUSE LANE. A party worked by day and night repairing the road by BRIDGE No. 16. By day a party from this unit carried on with the revetting and the work towards DORMY HOUSE LANE, and another party supervised the infantry working party in the communication trench in the South Bank of ZILLEBEKE LAKE.	J.W.Reynoldson
Sept 14th & 15th & 16th & 17th	Parties from this unit supervised infantry working parties by night on the communication trench between MAPLE COPSE and the junction of REGENT & OXFORD STREETS, also on the supporting route via the MOATED GRANGE. By day a party carried on with revetting and laying trench boards in DORMY HOUSE LANE, and another party supervised the working party in the communication trench in the South Bank of ZILLEBEKE LAKE. Three carpenters were sent to report at G.17.b.10-5 for joining the hutting party on 14/9/15	J.W.Reynoldson

Army Form C. 2118.

WAR DIARY
or
INTELLIGENCE SUMMARY.
(Erase heading not required.)

Instructions regarding War Diaries and Intelligence Summaries are contained in F.S. Regs., Part II. and the Staff Manual respectively. Title pages will be prepared in manuscript.

Hour, Date, Place	Summary of Events and Information	Remarks and references to Appendices
Sheet No 3. Sept 1915. Sept 18, 19, 20, 21, 22nd	By night a party from this unit supplied the working party on the supporting posts near the MOATED GRANGE. By day, parties worked on the communication trench in the South Bank of ZILLEBEKE LAKE and on DORMY HOUSE LANE.	[signature] Haymlong
Sept 23rd	Work was carried on as above. In the evening II Lieut Watson went up to SANCTUARY WOOD with an N.C.O and made a reconnaissance of the German trenches in front of T8 & and C1.	[signature] Haymlong
Sept 24	2 Lieut Challenor and II Lieut Watson reported to the O.Cs of the Royal Scots, 4 Gordon Highlanders in the morning, and were instructed to be up in SANCTUARY WOOD with their sections before the bombardment commenced. 6 T8 and 4 Bangalore Torpedoes were made at the billets, and were sent up to SANCTUARY WOOD in the evening. 2 Lieut Halsall with a party of 1 NCO and 4 sappers marched out of billets at 7pm and reported to G.O.C. 9th Infantry Brigade at MAPLE COPSE and was instructed to report to the O.C Royal Scots Fusiliers in SANCTUARY WOOD, taking two Bangalow Torpedoes. The O.C Company went up to MAPLE COPSE with this party, and reported to G.O.C. 8th Infantry Brigade, and was instructed to stand by. The O.C Company formed a combined the Suffolk Head quarters in MAPLE COPSE.	[signature] Haymlong

Forms/C. 2118/10
(B 29 6) W 4141—463 100,000 9/14 H W V

WAR DIARY or INTELLIGENCE SUMMARY

Army Form C. 2118

Hour, Date, Place	Summary of Events and Information	Remarks and references to Appendices
Sheet N° 4 Sept 1915 Sept 24th (continued)	Sections N°s 1 & 3 under Lieut Williams, with II Lieut Dobie marched out & halted at 8.30 p.m. until tin hat carts and proceeded to the Ramparts at YPRES, where accommodation had been allotted. Lieut Challener in charge of N° 4 Section left billets at 11 pm and reported to M.O.C. 2nd Royal Scots at 1.45 am on the 25th in SANCTUARY WOOD. II Lieut Watson in charge of N° 2 Section left billets at 11 pm and took up their position in SANCTUARY WOOD at 2 am on the morning of the 25th.	
Sept 25th	Lieut Challener had been instructed by the O.C. Royal Scots to divide his Section into two groups. One group was instructed to follow up B Company and to help to consolidate the captured trenches, and the other group to follow C Company and to do the same. Our N.C.O. and sappers were detailed to assist a working party of 2nd Royal Scots in opening up communication between our own and the captured trenches. At 4.20 am after the bombardment the parties went forward with the second attacking line and reached the German 3rd line trenches, and assisted to consolidate same. Lieut Challener came back from the German trench to ascertain what progress was being made with the communication trench. Lieut Challener then returned to the captured trenches, and guided up a supporting party of 2nd Royal Scots. An attempt was made to open up communication back from the German trenches but the work was very slow on account of the very heavy shelling.	

WAR DIARY or INTELLIGENCE SUMMARY

Hour, Date, Place	Summary of Events and Information	Remarks and references to Appendices
Sheet No 5 Sept 1915 Sept 25	2nd Lieut Watson in charge of No 2 Section had his section divided up in two groups. One group under Lieut Gell of Lt 2nd Royal Scots were to open up communication from the assembly trench in front of B8 to the German lines. The other group under 2nd Lieut Watson was to open up communication between the Capper dir and the captured trenches. 2nd Lieut Watson and his men went out before the bombardment to a wire in front of the German lines. After the attacking party went forward 2nd Lieut Watson and his ½ Section together with a working party of 4th Gordons started to dig a communication trench towards the German lines, and in two hours, under very heavy shell fire, 80 yards was dug. 2nd Lieut Watson telephoned to the adjutant of 1st/4th Gordons informing him that there were 18 casualties in the working party, and was told to go forward and assist in consolidating the captured trenches. Shortly afterwards 1st/4th Gordons retired, and Lt Cappns was asked to dig up during the retirement. 2nd Lieut Watson then took charge of 25 men of 1st/4th Gordons in B8, as there was no other officer there, and remained with them until they were relieved.	[signature]

Army Form C. 2118

WAR DIARY
or
INTELLIGENCE SUMMARY.
(Erase heading not required.)

Instructions regarding War Diaries and Intelligence Summaries are contained in F.S. Regs., Part II. and the Staff Manual respectively. Title pages will be prepared in manuscript.

Hour, Date, Place	Summary of Events and Information	Remarks and references to Appendices
Sheet No 6 Sept 14/15. Sept 15	Lieut Halsall and his party were instructed by the O.C Royal Scots Fusiliers to demolish wire and undergrowth in the place on the enemy's front with Bangalore Torpedoes, which was to be exploded simultaneously with the mine. The Torpedoes were put out, and as there was only one exploder available, one was exploded at 4.15 a.m. and at 4.15½ a.m. Lieut Halsall afterwards reported to H.O.C Royal Scots Fusiliers and was informed that his party was not required (and further on the then reported) was at MAPLE COPSE. The 9.O.C 9th Infantry Brigade informed me that Lieut Halsall and his party could return to billets. Lieut Challans and II Lieut Watson with parts of their sections reported to at MAPLE COPSE, and I was instructed by the 9.O.C 8th Infantry Brigade to send them back to billets. At 6 p.m. Capton Harris was instructed by the 9.O.C 8th Infantry Brigade to report to H.O.C. Royal Scots, with a view to arranging work to be done by howitzing parties that night. Major Enfield of the 4th South Lancs, and Lieut Williams of this unit met me there, and we inspected our front line. Sections No 1 to 3, which had been in reserve, were employed in wiring in front of B 4, 18 and returned to billets in the morning of the 2 gr.	[signature]

Army Form C. 2118

WAR DIARY
or
INTELLIGENCE SUMMARY.
(Erase heading not required.)

Instructions regarding War Diaries and Intelligence Summaries are contained in F. S. Regs., Part II. and the Staff Manual respectively. Title pages will be prepared in manuscript.

Hour, Date, Place	Summary of Events and Information	Remarks and references to Appendices
Sheet No. 4 Sept 1915.	The total casualties is billed, wounded and missing amounts to 15 N.C.O.s & men.	Ploegsteert
Sept 25th		
Sept 26th	Company rested in billets	Ploegsteert
Sept 27th	Section No. 1 & 3 together with one section of the East Riding Field Co. were employed during the night in wiring and consolidating our position.	Ploegsteert
Sept 28th, 29th & 30th	By night a party from this unit wired in front of our trenches, and another party together with two sections of the East Riding Field Co. RE worked on the parapet of DORMY HOUSE LANE, and another party on the repair to the transport road from KRUISSTRAAT to ZILLEBEKE. By day a party from this unit, together with the E.R. section of the East Riding Field Co. RE, worked on the dressing station at KRUISSTRAAT.	Ploegsteert
	One sapper wounded at KRUISSTRAAT, while returning from work on 30th	Ploegsteert

121/7437

3rd Fontain

1/1 Cheshire Fd Coy R.E.

Oct 1915

Vol IX.

WAR DIARY
or
INTELLIGENCE SUMMARY.
(Erase heading not required.)

Army Form C. 2118

Instructions regarding War Diaries and Intelligence Summaries are contained in F. S. Regs., Part II. and the Staff Manual respectively. Title pages will be prepared in manuscript.

Hour, Date, Place	Summary of Events and Information	Remarks and references to Appendices
Oct 1915 Sheet N° 1		
Oct 1st	The whole of the available men of this unit, together with two sections of the East Riding Field Co which are attached to this unit were employed during the night on wiring in front of our trenches in SANCTUARY WOOD. A party were employed in billets in preparing cases for its charges necessary to demolish bridges from N° 12 to 18 inclusive. One casualty in this unit.	J. Haynhurst Major R.E.(T)
Oct 2nd	Repairs were carried out to the syphon at ZILLEBEKE LAKE. All available men from this unit and one section of East Riding Field Co(attached) were employed on wiring our front line, by night. Work was continued in cases for demolition of Bridges 12 to 18.	J. Haynhurst Major R.E.(T)
Oct 3rd	By day a party was employed on repairs to roof and drains of flooring in advanced dressing Station in MAPLE COPSE, and another party was employed on the railway between MAPLE COPSE and ZILLEBEKE. By night all available men, with one Section of East Riding Field Co R.E. worked on wiring our parapet line in SANCTUARY WOOD.	J. Haynhurst Major R.E.(T)
Oct 4th	By night all available men from this unit, with one section of the East Riding Field R.E. were wiring in front of our trenches in SANCTUARY WOOD.	J. Haynhurst Major R.E.(T)
Oct 5th	By day one party from this unit worked on broken gun emplacement in SANCTUARY WOOD, and party from this unit with the Section of the East Riding Field Co R.E. worked on the parapet of ZILLEBEKE STREET. By day a party from this unit worked on the railway from ZILLEBEKE to SANCTUARY WOOD.	J. Haynhurst Major R.E.(T)

WAR DIARY
or
INTELLIGENCE SUMMARY
(Erase heading not required.)

Army Form C. 2118.

Hour, Date, Place	Summary of Events and Information	Remarks and references to Appendices
Oct 1915 (Sheet No 2)		
Oct 6th	By day a section of this unit were employed on repairing the railway between MAPLE COPSE and ZILLEBEKE. By night a party from this unit worked on a machine gun emplacement in SANCTUARY WOOD. A section of the 103rd Field Coy arrived from billets, having been attached for instruction.	[signature] Major RE(T)
Oct 7th & 8th	By day a party from this unit worked on roadway between ZILLEBEKE and SANCTUARY WOOD, and a mixed party from this unit and the section of the 103rd Field Coy attached started bomb stores in MAPLE COPSE. By night a party from this unit and the 103rd Field Coy worked on machine gun emplacement in SANCTUARY WOOD. By night another party from this unit, with members of the 103rd Field RE and a section of the East Riding Field RE worked on the parapet of ZILLEBEKE STREET.	[signature]
Oct 9th	By day the section of the East Riding Field RE attached to this unit worked on the parapet of ZILLEBEKE STREET, and a party from this unit and the 103rd Field RE worked on the machine gun emplacement in SANCTUARY WOOD; another party from this unit repaired road of No 16. By day mixed parties from this unit and the 103rd Field RE worked on the bomb stores in MAPLE COPSE, and preparing forward billets at ZILLEBEKE. The section of the 103rd Field Coy returned to its unit, and another section was attached for instruction.	[signature]

Army Form C. 2118.

SHEET No 3.

WAR DIARY
or
INTELLIGENCE SUMMARY.
(Erase heading not required.)

Instructions regarding War Diaries and Intelligence Summaries are contained in F.S. Regs., Part II. and the Staff Manual respectively. Title pages will be prepared in manuscript.

Hour, Date, Place	Summary of Events and Information	Remarks and references to Appendices
October 10th	A party from this unit worked by day on the Bomb Store in MAPLE COPSE and another party preparing forward billets in ZILLEBEKE. A further portion of this unit was marked out. The usual party patrolled SANCTUARY WOOD and the railway from ZILLEBEKE to SANCTUARY WOOD and carried out any necessary repairs. By night. A party from this unit carried out small repairs needed on Bridge 6. A mixed party from this unit & 103 Fld Coy worked on machine gun emplacement in SANCTUARY WOOD.	Glo. ypeducy
Oct 11 to 12th	A party from this unit continued work by day on the bomb store in MAPLE COPSE also on forward billets at ZILLEBEKE and continuing working out of new trench. Machine gun loopholes & snipers loopholes were made at billets. By night. A party from this unit continued work on M.G. emplacement in SANCTUARY WOOD. A mixed party from this unit & East Riding Fld Co worked on railway between ZILLEBEKE & SANCTUARY WOOD.	Glo. ypeducy
Oct 13th	Worked and continued on bomb store at MAPLE COPSE & forward billets at ZILLEBEKE. Also a party from this unit supervised infantry working on new trench in SANCTUARY WOOD. By night. Two parties from this unit worked on M.G. emplacements in SANCTUARY WOOD. The section of the East Riding Fld Co. attached to this unit worked on the Railway to SANCTUARY WOOD.	Glo. ypeducy

SHEET No. 4.

WAR DIARY
INTELLIGENCE SUMMARY.
(Erase heading not required.)

Army Form C. 2118.

Hour, Date, Place	Summary of Events and Information	Remarks and references to Appendices
October 14th	A party from this unit worked on tombstone in MAPLE COPSE. Another party started making a sample deep dug-out in new trench in SANCTUARY WOOD. Carpenters working on mining case trench boards.	J.Gwynhugen
15th	By night a party from this unit worked on M.G. emplacement in SANCTUARY WOOD and the section of East Riding C.R.E. works on railway up to Sanctuary Wood. An officer & party from this unit supervised working party from Entrenching Battalion working on supporting points near ZILLEBEKE. (N of ZILLEBEKE LAKE)	
Oct 16th	A party from this unit completed the tombstone in MAPLE COPSE to-day. A party also worked on the deep dug-out.	J.Gwynhugen
17th	The section of East Riding Field Co. were employed on revetting the new trench in SANCTUARY WOOD. Work was continued on forward billets at ZILLEBEKE. By night a party from this unit patrolled & repaired the railway from ZILLEBEKE to SANCTUARY WOOD and a party worked on the dugouts in the supporting points near ZILLEBEKE	
18th	A party from this Coy. patrolled & improved the tram line between ZILLEBEKE & SANCTUARY WOOD. Work was also continued on the new trench in SANCTUARY WOOD and on the deep dug-out. Also on forward billets near ZILLEBEKE. N.Co. 41 man was sent to SANCTUARY WOOD for a further 3 days to assist infantry in drainage of front line trenches. Box drains, trench boards etc. were made at back billets.	J.Gwynhugen
19th	A party from attached section of East Riding Co.R.E. patrolled & repaired the tram line by night. By day – Work was continued on deep dug out & also on forward billets at ZILLEBEKE. A mixed party from this unit of East Riding Co. Works on revetting Trench boards, M.G. emplacements in new trench in SANCTUARY WOOD, mining cases etc. were made at back billets.	J.Gwynhugen

Army Form C. 2118

SHEET No 5 WAR DIARY or INTELLIGENCE SUMMARY.

(Erase heading not required.)

Instructions regarding War Diaries and Intelligence Summaries are contained in F. S. Regs., Part II. and the Staff Manual respectively. Title pages will be prepared in manuscript.

Hour, Date, Place 1915	Summary of Events and Information	Remarks and references to Appendices
October 20th	A party from this unit patrols & repairs the tram line (nightly) between ZILLEBEKE & SANCTUARY WOOD. By day 2 sections of this Coy. worked in new trench in SANCTUARY WOOD, on deep dugout, M.G. emplacement & revetting. Attacks section of East Riding Co. worked on forward billets at ZILLEBEKE. Trench boards, mining cases etc. were made at back billets.	Glaynchny
21st	By night a party from E. Riding Co. patrolled & repaired the tram line. By day 2 sections of Coy. worked on new trench in SANCTUARY WOOD. An officer & 2 men of the Coy. supervised extension of C.T. on North side of ZILLEBEKE LAKE. Orders were received that the Coy. was to move tomorrow as the Divn. is being relieved by 17th Divn. R.E. Stores in possession of Coy. were returned to R.E. Park.	Glaynchny
22nd	Two officers of this Coy. accompanied officers of 17th Field Coy. & showed them over all work in hand. At 5.30 p.m. Coy. marched out from billets and proceeded to Rest billets at STEENVOORDE (J.36.c.7.8. – ref Sheet 28. 1/40,000 Belgium & Part of France). Arrived in these billets at 1.0 a.m. on 23rd.	Glaynchny
23rd	Coy. employed in erecting shelters & generally cleaning up & improving billets which are very overcrowded.	Glaynchny
24th	General fatigues in billets. An inspection of clothing & equipment was held.	Glaynchny
25th	Owing to wet weather, no work, except necessary fatigues, was done.	Glaynchny

WAR DIARY or INTELLIGENCE SUMMARY.

SHEET No. 6.

Army Form C. 2118.

Instructions regarding War Diaries and Intelligence Summaries are contained in F. S. Regs., Part II. and the Staff Manual respectively. Title pages will be prepared in manuscript.

(Erase heading not required.)

Hour, Date, Place	Summary of Events and Information	Remarks and references to Appendices
October 26th	Dismounted sections – Squad drill, company drill, physical drill + musketry. Mounted Section – Riding + driving drill. 4 men of this Bgd. detailed to take part in the parade on 27th for inspection by H.M. The King – reported to C.R.E. offices at 3 p.m.	Locre huts / Locre huts
27th to 31st.	Company training in rest billets.	Locre huts
	APPENDIX "A".	
	On night of October 21st, a party from this unit, by orders of G.O.C. 3rd Divn, removes the weather vane from the top of the belfry of ZILLEBEKE CONVENT and sent same to H.Q. 3rd Divn (REMINGHELST)	Locre huts

3rd Dn

1/ Cheshire P. Co. R.E.

Nov. / roe X

12/7663

3rd Division

Army Form C. 2118.

WAR DIARY
or
INTELLIGENCE SUMMARY.
(Erase heading not required.)

Sheet No 1.

Hour, Date, Place	Summary of Events and Information	Remarks and references to Appendices
November 1915 1st to 4th.	Company training carried out in Rear Billets - Section - Company and Physical Drill.	J.Waynehuyser Major. RE(T)
5th.	The Coy. paraded at full strength and was inspected by the G.O.C. II Army. The following N.C.O.s and Men received Cards in respect of their having been mentioned in despatches for good service in the field :- 63. C.S.M. Quigley T. R. 4. Sergt. Armstrong J. 523. Corp. Hyison B.H. 11. Lnc.Corp. Hughes E.	
6.	A party of 8 Joiners was detailed to erect a stand for the presentation of French Decorations in Steenwoorde. A general holiday having been granted by the G.O.C. no other work done beyond fatigues -	J.Waynehuyser Major RE(T)
7th.	Sunday. Fatigues only.	J.Waynehuyser Major RE(T)
8th.	A party of 2 Officers. 12 N.C.O.s was detailed to assist with the Instruction of Infantry attending the Pioneer School. The work covering instructional training of dug outs, machine gun emplacements, blockhouses and wiring. The instruction included various forms of	J.Waynehuyser Major RE(T)

WAR DIARY or INTELLIGENCE SUMMARY.

Army Form C. 2118.

Hour, Date, Place	Summary of Events and Information	Remarks and references to Appendices
November 1915. 8th cont.	continued drainage and fascining of trenches. One section was detailed to work on permanent horse standings. Remainder of Coy. did Coy. training, physical drill. The following men received cards in respect of their having been mentioned to Brigadier for their work and conduct in the field on the 25th Sept 1915:— 508 Sapper Simm H. S 63 Sapper Swinbank G.B.	J.Wayne Major RE(?)
9th to 13th.	Work and training as for the 8th.	J.Wayne Major RE
14th.	Note. On the 13th 5th Corps H.Q. wired to say that 2/Lt. G.F. Watson had attained the D.S.O. for his conspicuous conduct in the field on the 25th Sept. 1915. Sunday. The whole Coy. paraded at 11 am on Coy. Parade Ground for Divine Service. Except for fatigues no work was done.	J.Wayne Major RE
15th.	A party sent as usual to instruct at the Pioneer School. The remainder of Coy. carried out Coy Training.	J.Wayne Major RE
16th.	Work and Training as for the 15th.	

WAR DIARY or INTELLIGENCE SUMMARY.

Army Form C. 2118.

Sheet No 3

(Erase heading not required.)

Hour, Date, Place	Summary of Events and Information	Remarks and references to Appendices
November 1915 17th	Work and Training as for the 16th except that an additional party of 8 N.C.Os was sent to Infantry Batt. HQrs to instruct in Gabion making.	Slayneburgen Major R.E.(?)
18th	Parties to Pioneer School + Inf. HQrs. again sent out and the section of Carpenters being occupied in making Tables, Forms, Blackboards &c for Officers Training School. Remainder did Coy Training.	J.Slayneburgen Major R.E.(?)
19th	All Carpenters continued work on School furniture. Remainder marched for Route March covering 11 miles in 3 hrs. 50 mins. (including total halting time of 1hr 15 mins) without exertion.	Slayneburgen Major R.E.(?)
20th	2 Officers detailed to supervise clearing up of Pioneer School and removal of material to R.E. Parts. Carpenters continued work on furniture. Remainder carried out Coy Training.	J.Slayneburgen Major R.E.(?)
21st	Sunday. Carpenters continued work on furniture. Coy attended Divine Service & a good number remained for Holy Communion. No other work carried out.	Slayneburgen Major R.E.(?)
22nd	A party of 1 N.C.O. 5 Sappers was sent to meet material from Pioneer School to 24th Div. R.E. Parts Diekebush. The remainder of Coy was employed on fatigues and preparation for leaving billet.	Slayneburgen Major R.E.(?)
23rd	In accordance with orders marched out at 7.30 am from Reninghelst and proceeded to Ouderdom where it arrived at 3.30 pm. and relieved the 104th Field Coy R.E. whose quarters it took over. Map reference. G.36.a.7.4. Sheet 28. 1/40000 scale Belgium and France.  Slayneburgen Major R.E.(?)

Army Form C. 2118.

Sheet No. 4

WAR DIARY
or
INTELLIGENCE SUMMARY.

(Erase heading not required.)

Instructions regarding War Diaries and Intelligence Summaries are contained in F. S. Regs., Part II. and the Staff Manual respectively. Title pages will be prepared in manuscript.

Hour, Date, Place	Summary of Events and Information	Remarks and references to Appendices
November 1915 24th	A party of 1 Officer and No 2 Section commenced the laying out and erection of a new Saw Mill of Reining witr. A party of 1 N.C.O. and 12 Sappers with 3 Pontoon wagons were engaged in drawing timber from wood (A8 c 4.5) for the Saw Mill. The Remainder of Coy. carried out fatigues and straightening up of billets. No 1 and 3 Section paraded at 5.30 pm under their Officers and proceeded to forward billets in Scottish Wood. The following N.C.O.s received cards in recognition of their conduct in the field on the 25th Sept. 1915:- 527. L/Corp. Barker R. awarded the D.C.M. 552 Corp. Martin J. Mentioned in despatches.	J. Wayne Major RE(?)
25th	One Section continued with erection of Saw Mill at Reninghlst and laying of tramways to Same. Two Pontoon wagons with loading party drew wood from A.8.c.4.5:- The G.S. wagon went to M. 18 a 2.8. for Sand. The Forward Sections worked on their billets in Scottish Wood.	J. Wayne Major RE(?)

Sheet No 5.

WAR DIARY
or
INTELLIGENCE SUMMARY.

(Erase heading not required.)

Army Form C. 2118

Hour, Date, Place	Summary of Events and Information	Remarks and references to Appendices
November 1915. 26.	No 2 Section and Officer carried on with erection of Sausages & Runing shelter and making of roads. A party of 2 N.C.Os 5 Sappers were detailed to work with Divisional Hutting Party. Forward Section. No 1 and 3 worked on the O.T. to Bois Confluent. Pickets for revetting were made in forward letter. Assistance by supervision was given to the garrison of front line trenches in improving same.	J Haynebayne Major R.E.O
27.	No 2 Section and Officer continued work on Saw Mill and road at Ruing hilst. An Officer went to and advised on timber construction at the Grenade School. Two motor wagons with loading party drew timber from wood A B C 45. Forward Section. 6 N.C.Os and men assisted Royal Scots Position in improving fire trenches. The party worked on improving the O.T. to Bois Confluent. Another carried on work on railway from Scottish Wood towards E Agenville.	J Haynebayne Major R.E(I)

Sheet No 6

WAR DIARY
or
INTELLIGENCE SUMMARY.
(Erase heading not required.)

Army Form C. 2118.

Hour, Date, Place	Summary of Events and Information	Remarks and references to Appendices
November 1915 28th.	No 2 Section and Officer continued work on Sawmill and road at Rening huts. Two pontoon wagons with loading party proceeded to Wood Aceus and drew timber. Forward Sections. 8 N.C.Os and men assisted and drilled the infantry in improving the front line trenches. A party from the unit took assisted by the 4th South Lancs. worked on the C.T. to Bois Confluent. Another party assisted by out from 4th South Lancs. worked on the railway from Drake walk to Bois Confluent. Three men worked on dwelling places.	J.Wayne Morgan Major REP
Nov 29th 1915 Nov 30th 1915	As above, except that 3 men were detailed to supervise infantry working party making French pattern dugouts in SCOTTISH WOOD	J.Wayne Morgan Major REP J.Wayne Morgan Major REP

Christine P. Croft.   See X/ad

3d Div.

Army Form C. 2118.

WAR DIARY
or
INTELLIGENCE SUMMARY.
(Erase heading not required.)

SHEET 1.

Hour, Date, Place	Summary of Events and Information	Remarks and references to Appendices
December 1st.	One section of the Coy made and officer worked on the erection of Sawmill at RENINGHELST. Forward Sections - A party assisted & advised the infantry with work on front trenches, building french dug-outs. A small party supervised infantry building french dug-outs. A party assisted by party from 4th South Lancs continued laying french tramline to Bois CONFLUENT. A party worked with 4th S. Lancs on Main C.T. to " " Nos 2nd Sections relieved No 1+3 Sections at forward billets this evening	J. Wayneburger Major.
December 2nd & 3rd.	Work was continued as usual on Sawmill at RENINGHELST. Forward Sections continued work as usual i.e. on french tramline, Main C.T. to Bois CONFLUENT, assisting infantry in front line, & supervising infantry building french dug-outs. Billets also prepared pickets &c for revetting of Main C.T.	J. Soupeburger Major.
December 4th.	Work was continued as usual on Saw Mill at RENINGHELST. Forward Sections continued work as usual on french tramline, Main C.T., assisting infantry in front line & supervising infantry building french dug-outs. A Small party continued building special emplacements in front-line trenches.	J. Wayneburger Major.
December 5th.	Work was continued on Saw Mill at RENINGHELST. Forward sections continued work on Main C.T. assisting infantry in front trenches supervising infantry building french dug-outs, also building special emplacements in front line. The french railway having now reached a point where it is considered inadvisable to work in daylight work on same was continued tonight. 1 N Co. H Sapper assisted the infantry today in building M.G. emplacement in front line. Work was also commenced tonight on a M.G. emplacement in Bus House (Near St. Eloi)	J. Wayneburger Major.

Army Form C. 2118.

WAR DIARY
INTELLIGENCE SUMMARY.   SHEET 2.
(Erase heading not required.)

Hour, Date, Place	Summary of Events and Information	Remarks and references to Appendices
December 6th to 7th	Work was continued on Saw Mill at RENINGHELST. Boxes for special emplacement, also revetting pickets were made at billets. Forward Sections - by night - a party worked on laying of French railway (assisted by 4th South Lancs). A small party assisted by 4th Sloans continued work on M.G. emplacement in BusHouse. By day - parties worked as usual on Main C.T. to Bois Confluent, building special emplacements in front line, assisting infantry in front trenches, and on M.G. emplacement in front line, & supervising infantry building french dug-outs.	J.Waynehouven Major.
December 8th (C.R.E.)	Work was continued on Saw Mill at RENINGHELST. Boxes for special emplacements were made at billets also revetting pickets. A party was employed on drainage at billets. Forward Sections - work same as for 6th & 7th with No.1 & 3 Sections relieved No.2 & 4 Sections this evening. A draft of 13 men (4 NCO's, 8 sappers & 1 driver) to form a Searchlight section, joined this Coy. to-day.	J.Waynehouven Major.
December 9th	Work was continued as usual on SawMill, Boxes for special emplacements, Revetting pickets, & drainage at billets. Forward Sections - Work as usual i.e. on trench railway & M.G. emplacement in BusHouse by night & by day on Main C.T., building special emplacements in front line, assisting infantry with work in front line & M.G. emplacement in front line & supervising infantry building french dug-outs.	J.Waynehouven Major.

WAR DIARY

INTELLIGENCE SUMMARY

(Erase heading not required.)

Army Form C. 2118

SHEET No. 3

Place	Date 1915	Hour	Summary of Events and Information	Remarks and references to Appendices
(J. Bloc.) Ypres	Dec: 10th and 11th		Work was continued on the Saw Mill at RENINGHELST. A party under an officer with a party of Officers NCOs of 13th Kenya (Kpoe) Regt. in entrenching, revetting etc. "Forward Sections" – Work was continued the same as yesterday (9th) at WEBB	Moynihan Major
	12th		Work was continued on Saw Mill & picks & trenchboards were made at billets. Forward Sections – Work same as for Dec 10th/11th with the addition that work was continued on M.G. emplacement at Bos House by day (as well as by night) tunnelling from the dugouts to the emplacement.	Moynihan Major
	13th 14th			
	15th		Work for Back Sections the same as usual. Forward Sections – Work was continued as usual. The M.G. emplacement at Bos House was completed. Also a small party worked by day repairing Right Battn H.Q. dugouts. No. 4 Section relieved No. 3 in forward billets this evening.	Moynihan Major
	16th to 17th to 18th		Back Sections – Work as usual. Forward Sections – Work was continued on the trench railway also on the M.G. emplacement at Bos House (Strengthening the dugouts). On the Main C.T. to Bois CONFLUENT, assisting infantry with work in front trenches, supervising infantry building French dugouts. Also by night, parties supervised infantry working parties retrieving trenches R2 & Q2	Moynihan Major
	19th		Owing to a gas attack delivered against our trenches near WIELTJE at 6.20 a.m. to "Stand by". This order was cancelled at 11.15 a.m. Work then proceeded as usual. Forward Sections – Work was continued by night on the railway; supervising infantry Working parties on trenches Q2 & R2; a second M.G. emplacement was commenced at Bos House by day. A party assisted the infantry to build French dugouts at Left Battn H.Q. A party worked on the Main C.T. to Bois CONFLUENT. A party assisted the infantry with work in the front trenches. A party supervised infantry building French dugouts.	Moynihan Major
	20th		Back & Forward Sections – Work same as on the 19th.	Moynihan

Army Form C. 2118

WAR DIARY
INTELLIGENCE SUMMARY
(Erase heading not required.)

SHEET No. 4.

Instructions regarding War Diaries and Intelligence Summaries are contained in F. S. Regs., Part II. and the Staff Manual respectively. Title Pages will be prepared in manuscript.

Place	Date 1915	Hour	Summary of Events and Information	Remarks and references to Appendices
Ypres (S.Sec.)	Dec. 21st		Back Sections - Work was continued on the sawmill at RENINGHELST. Parties at TILLEB made trench boards & pickets, also tables & benches for III Divl. Rest Station. Forward Sections - By night parties worked on the railway & the second M.G. emplacement at Bus House. By day parties worked on the main C.T. building - special emplacement in front trenches; assisting infantry with work in front trenches; assisting infantry to build steel dug-outs at Left Batn H.Q. & supervising infantry building French dug-outs in SCOTTISH WOOD. No 1 Section relieved No. 2 section in forward billets this evening.	Magurahm Major
	22nd		Back & Forward Sections - Work same as for 21st. No. 3 Section relieves No. 4 this evening.	Magurahm Major
	23rd & 24th		Back Sections - Work was continued on the sawmill. Tables, benches & trackboards were made at billets. A party instructs officers & NCO's of 13th King's (L'pool) Regt in fieldworks. Forward Sections - By day - work same as for 22nd. By night - work same as for 22nd + also Parties supervised infantry working on trench R2.	Magurahm Major
	25th & 26th & 27th		Back Sections - Work was continued on Saw Mill. Tables & benches were made at billets. Forward Sections - Work - same as for 24th. for III Divl. Rest Station.	Magurahm Major
	28th		Work for Back & Forward Sections - same as for 27th. No. 2 Section relieved No. 1 Section at Forward billets this evening.	Magurahm Major
	29th		Back Sections - Work same as usual. Forward Sections. A wind was in a dangerous quarter (between E.&S.) "Gas standby" precautions were observed & no working parties left billets today or in the evening. All men worked on trench dug-outs in SCOTTISH WOOD. No 4 Section relieved No. 3 Section this evening in forward billets at SCOTTISH WOOD.	Magurahm Major

WAR DIARY

INTELLIGENCE SUMMARY

(Erase heading not required.)

Army Form C. 2118

SHEET N° 5.

Place: Ypres (St. B.C.)

Date 1915	Hour	Summary of Events and Information	Remarks and references to Appendices
Dec 30th		Back Sections - work as usual. i.e. on the Saw mill & making trenchboards at billets. Also tables & benches for III Div Rest Station. Forward Sections. The wire being changed to S.W. again during the night. work was continued as usual. i.e. by night on the decon M.G. emplacement at Bus House, on the railway & supervising infantry working on rebuilding trench R2. By day - On the main C.T. to Bois Confluent, assisting infantry in front trenches, & supervising infantry building second line, and.	[signature] Major
31st		Back & Forward Sections - work same as for 30th.	[signature] Major

3rd Divisional Engineers.

1/1st CHESHIRE FIELD COMPANY R.E.

JANUARY 1 9 1 6.

Army Form C. 2118
Sheet 1.

WAR DIARY
or
INTELLIGENCE SUMMARY
(Erase heading not required.)

Place	Date	Hour	Summary of Events and Information	Remarks and references to Appendices
Ypres (S. Eloi)	January 1916 1st		<u>Back Section</u> One section worked in Sawmill at Businghelst. Parties at billets worked on Tables and benches for III Division Rear Camp. Also trench boards and pickets. <u>Forward Section</u> By night parties worked, assisted by infantry, on front trenches. The M.G. emplacement at BUS HOUSE and light railway. The M.G. emplacement at BOIS CONFLUENT C.T. and the front line trenches also worked. By day parties working on french dugouts in SCOTTISH WOOD. The following Officers NCOs and Men were mentioned in Despatch in this date :- Lieut. H.A. HALSALL Lieut. G.F. WATSON. D.S.O. 63 CSM. TR QUIGLEY " Sergt. H.J. ARMSTRONG. 523 Corpl. J.W.H. HIGSON. 552 " J. MARTIN 11 L/Corp. F. HUGHES. 527 " R. BARKER. D.C.M 331. Sapper. G.W. JONES. 508 " H. SIMS. 563 " G.B. SWINBANK	Previous Messages Major R.E.(T)

WAR DIARY
or
INTELLIGENCE SUMMARY

(Erase heading not required.)

Army Form C. 2118

Sheet 2.

Place	Date	Hour	Summary of Events and Information	Remarks and references to Appendices
	January 1916			
	2		**Back Section.** The section worked on Sawmill at Reninghelst. Made tables and benches for III Div. Rest Camp also trench boards and pickets.	
			Forward Section. By night work as for the 1st was continued with. The light railway being connected up to the existing line at DEAD DOG FARM. By day work was carried on in the front line trenches, BOIS CONFLUENT C.T. and French dugouts in SCOTTISH WOOD, also a frame for Officers dugout for fire line was completed.	
	3		Work was continued as usual on Sawmill at Reninghelst. The section at killers in addition to Table & trenches constructed special emplacement boxes and worked on drainage around killer. No.1 Section relieved No.2 Section on Forward Billets.	
			Forward Section. By night parties as usual worked on front trenches. They continued to ballast BUSHOUSE emplacement and the railway which they continued with. By day in addition to the work of the 2nd, which was continued with, a party took up material and prepared a special emplacement in R.3. Work at Sawmill and exactly as for the 3rd was continued with.	
	4		**Forward Sections.** By night a party supervised infantry on front trenches and continued ballasting railway also relaying wooden curves of correct gauge. A small party worked on BUSHOUSE which is now ready for use though still in an incomplete state. By day a party laid tripoints and curves of a switch for new light railway to the R.F.A. lines. Parties assisted infantry in front line trenches. In BOIS CONFLUENT C.T. and dug outs in SCOTTISH WOOD. Another party was employed in adjusting gauge of wooden laid curves.	J Bryce Burgon Major R.E.(T)

Army Form C. 2118

Sheet 3.

WAR DIARY
or
INTELLIGENCE SUMMARY
(Erase heading not required.)

Place	Date	Hour	Summary of Events and Information	Remarks and references to Appendices
YPRES - (ST. ELOI.)	January 1916 5.		Work proceeded at Sawmill at Reninghelst and billets at on Mievron day. In the evening No. 4 was relieved by No. 3 Section at Forward billets. **Forward Section.** By night a party continued ballasting the rail way and adjusting curves. A party worked on M.G. emplacement at BUS HOUSE. By day, parties worked on BOIS CONFLUENT C.T. Special emplacement in front line French dugouts in SCOTTISH Wood. and R.F.A light railway while at billets men prepared dug out frames and material for front line trench work.	Map RE(?) Haynington
	6.		Work on Sawmill at Reninghelst and at billets proceeded as usual on Mievron day. **Forward Section.** By night a party was employed in ballasting F.T. R2 other parties carried on as usual on the light railway ballasting. BUSHOUSE M.G. emplacement. By day two men supervised the gunners working on R.F.A Railway and other parties were employed tracks on as on previous day.	
	7.		Work on Sawmill at Reninghelst and at billets was continued as on Mievron day and a party was sent to SCOTTISH WOOD to assist infantry on French dugouts. **Forward Section.** By night a party continued work in front trenches laying trench boards opening parapet for sand bagging. Parties ballasted the railway and continued on BUSHOUSE M.G. emplacement. By day parties assisted infantry in front line trenches, the gunners on R.F.A. Rly. and completed the special emplacement in R3. also worked on Bois Confluent C.T. the men arrived at French Dug Out building at VOORMEZEELE.	

WAR DIARY or INTELLIGENCE SUMMARY

Army Form C. 2118
Sheet H.

Place	Date	Hour	Summary of Events and Information	Remarks and references to Appendices
YPRES. (ST. ELOI)	January 1916 8th		Work on Sawmill at Reninghelst and back billets continued as on previous day, a party being sent to forward billets to work on French dugouts, and 1 RFA. Railway. Forward Section, work continued exactly as for 7th by day and night.	Reconnaissance Major H.
	9th		Work on Sawmill and at back billets continued as on previous day. Forward Section. All working parties & work carried out exactly as on 8th & 7th.	
	10th		Work at Sawmill and at back billets same as previous days. In the evening No 2 Section relieved No 1 Section at Forward billets. Forward Section, All working parties same as for 8th & 7th by day but in addition by night two men worked on a Traverse in front line.	
	11th		Work on Sawmill and at back billets same as previous days but men working at the new Divisional Theatre. In the evening No 4 Section relieved No 3 Section at forward billets. Forward Section Parties worked by night on Bus HOUSE M.G. emplacement and in front line YP. Ken Chn. By day all working parties same as previous day.	
	12th		Work on Sawmill, back billets and Divisional Theatre same as on 11th. 1 N.C. Forward Section. One Officer + 2 N.C.O.s instructed a class of 4 O.C. in revetting at St Huberts halt. By night a party was employed at BUS HOUSE M.G. emplacement. By day all working parties same as previous day.	

WAR DIARY or INTELLIGENCE SUMMARY

Army Form C. 2118

Sheet 5.

(Erase heading not required.)

Instructions regarding War Diaries and Intelligence Summaries are contained in F. S. Regs., Part II. and the Staff Manual respectively. Title Pages will be prepared in manuscript.

Place	Date	Hour	Summary of Events and Information	Remarks and references to Appendices
Ypres (S. Eloi.)	January 1916 13th		Work on Sawmill at Reninghelst and took billets. Same as previous day while a party of 1 N.C.O. and 3 men was sent to SCOTTISH WOOD to supervise work on French dug outs. <u>Forward Sections.</u> By night parties worked on BUS HOUSE M.G. emplacement in P Trenches - The front line French R2. and assisted infantry on Engineer in P Trenches. - By day parties worked on the railway BOIS CONFLUENT C.T. and R.E.A. Railway. also French dug outs in SCOTTISH WOOD. -	Berryhurgess Major R.E.)
	14th.		Work on Sawmill. at took billets and parties sent out Same as 13th. <u>Forward Sections.</u> Parties by night worked on front trenches assisting infantry, BUSHOUSE M.G. emplacement and BOIS CONFLUEN C.T. also on P Trenches. By day, parties assisted infantry in the forward billets in BOIS CONFLUENT C.T. and remainder worked on dug outs in SCOTTISH WOOD. SCOTTISH WOOD was heavily shelled during the morning, the forward billets being hit and we suffered several casualties - (all wounded.) K two men evacuated to hospital being :- A Mud 1088 Sapper Davies E.T. 1142 " Lewis E.J. the man only bruised and returned to duty. The remainder being infantry.	
	15th.		Work same as for 14th. <u>Forward Section.</u> By night the same parties as on 14th. were sent out and the M.G. emplacement of BUS HOUSE was completed. By day work was carried on as on the 14th.	

WAR DIARY or INTELLIGENCE SUMMARY

Army Form C. 2118

Sheet 6.

(Erase heading not required.)

Place: S/Mas. (St. Eloi.)

Date	Hour	Summary of Events and Information	Remarks and references to Appendices
January 16th		Work on Sawmill at Ronninghelst and at Billets in Kruithoek and picket, carried out as usual. **Forward Section.** By night a party commenced laying knee-deep in O.3. and assisted the infantry in support the trench R2. A party was also employed repairing the railway which had been damaged by shell fire during the day. Another party supervised infantry in BOIS CONFLUENT C.T. By day a party assisted the infantry in fire line Kruches, another worked on special emplacements in R trenches. A new 60cm gauge line was put in Bollestbeck. All No.4 Section worked on dugouts in SCOTTISH WOOD.	Reconnaissance Map (attd)
17th		Work as for 16th but in addition a party drew timber from Abeele, two men worked at Divisional Theatre and two at Divisional Cinema. * **Forward Section.** Work by night and day as for 16th.	
		* No.5 No.1 Section relieved No.2 Section at Forward Billets	
18th		Work as for 16th was continued — No.3 Section relieved No.4 at Forward Billets. **Forward Section.** By night a party worked in Kruithoekstraat J. O2. By day work continued as for 16th and a dugout frame was made for sound staff in front line.	
19th		Work as for 16th and in addition a frame for concrete towers for R.F.A. O.P.s was started on. **Forward Section.** By night no work done due to reliefs being carried out. By day work done as for 16th.	

WAR DIARY / INTELLIGENCE SUMMARY

Army Form C. 2118
Sheet 7.

Place	Date	Hour	Summary of Events and Information	Remarks and references to Appendices
Ypres (S.B.)	January 1916. 20th		Work continued as usual on the dam will at RENINGHELST - parties worked on making frame for concrete O.P. also picket fthords for revetting. Forward Sections - By night - A party assisted the infantry working on trench R2. By day. 2 men assisted the R.E.A. laying a light railway. A party assisted the infantry in front trenches. A party assisted 13th Kings on BOIS CONFLUENT CT. Two men assisted infantry on building a new dressing station. Remainder continued work on "Trench dugouts" in SCOTTISH WOOD.	H. Bayntien Major
	21st to 22nd		Work continued same as for 20th. Forward Sections - Work as usual & in addition a party supervised infantry working party on BOIS CONFLUENT CT.	
	23rd		Work continued as usual. In addition a party made benches for 3 Div Rest Camp. Forward Section - By night - Work continued as on 22nd. By day.	
	24th		Back Sections continued work as on 23rd. Forward Section - By night - A party supervised infantry on BOIS CONFLUENT CT. A party laid trench boards in trench Q2. A party worked on trench railway - putting in sidings. By day - A party assisted the infantry in front trenches. A party assisted 13th Kings on BOIS CONFLUENT CT. A party worked on putting a siding in the railway in SCOTTISH WOOD. 2 men assisted R.F.A. on their light railway. Remainder worked on trench dugouts in SCOTTISH WOOD	
	25th to 26th		Back Section - A party worked on corduroy road round the stables. A party finished the benches for 3 Div Rest Camp and others were employed making trench frames. A party worked on Saw-mill at RENINGHELST. No 2 Section relieved No. 1 at forward billets. Forward Section - By night - A party continued putting sidings in the railway & a party continued laying trench boards in Q2. By day. Work continued same as for 24th.	

Army Form C. 2118

WAR DIARY
INTELLIGENCE SUMMARY
Sheet 8.
(Erase heading not required.)

Place	Date	Hour	Summary of Events and Information	Remarks and references to Appendices
Ypres (S.W.)	January 1916 27th		Back Sections continued work as usual. - Forward Sections - By Night - A party assisted 13th Kings working on trench R2 - a party on the railway commenced putting in a switch line between the VOORMEZEELE & BOIS CONFLUENT trench Rlys. By day - a party assisted infantry in front trenches. - A party assisted 13th Kings on BOIS CONFLUENT C.T. - 2 men assisted infantry building the new dressing station - 2 men assisted R.F.A. on their light railway. Remainder continued work on trench dug-outs in SCOTTISH WOOD.	Jaspho Innes Major RE
	28th		Back Sections continued work as usual - Forward Sections - By night - worked as on 27th with addition that 5 men supervised infantry party working on BOIS CONFLUENT C.T. By day. Work continued same as on 27th.	
	29th		Back Sections - A party supervised infantry building road. A party worked on the Corduroy rooms the stables - A party worked on the engines also the corduroy road at the saw mill. Forward Sections - By night - work continued same as for 28th. By day. Work continued as usual, with the addition that a small party commenced work at tillets making mine cases.	
	30th		Back Sections worked same as for 29th. Forward Sections. By night - Work as for 29th By day. Work as for 29th with addition that a small party commenced work on a concrete O.P. in the R.F.A. at MOATED GRANGE. No parties were sent to front trenches as wind was from E. to S.E.	
	31st		Back Sections - work as for 30th. Forward Sections. By night - work as for 30th with addition that 2 men commenced sinking a shaft for new exit to bombing pit in front of R3. By day. Work continues same as on 30th	

3rd Divisional Engineers

1/1ST CHESHIRE FIELD COMPANY R.E.

FEBRUARY 1916.

Army Form C. 2118

WAR DIARY
or
INTELLIGENCE SUMMARY
(Erase heading not required.)

Sheet 1 —

Place	Date	Hour	Summary of Events and Information	Remarks and references to Appendices
YPRES – (ST ELOI.)	February 1916 1st		Back Section. Parties worked on the engines and roads to Sawmill at REININGHELST, on corduroy road round horse lines, and assisted the Infantry building 1st Corps Signal dugouts near DICKEBUSCH ROAD. Forward Section. By night parties assisted the Infantry in front line Support trench Q2 — worked on watch tower up the VOORMEZEELE and BOIS CONFLUENT light railways which were completed — By day parties assisted the Infantry in front line "P" trenches, the 13th Kings L'pool Regt. in BROOKE AVENUE CT. Other parties worked on R.F.A. O.P. in MOATED GRANGE, Dressing Station near the Brasserie, new 1st Corps Signal dugout, the light Railways French dugouts in SCOTTISH WOOD. and a new exit for bombers in front line trench R3.	Fanshawe Major
	2nd and 3rd		Back Sections and Forward Sections. Work as for the 1st. except that by night parties worked on 1st Corps Signal dugout and laid duck boards in Q2.	
	4.		Back Section. Three were sent up to Forward Billets for Special work. Forward Section. With exception of 1 N.C.O. supervising Infantry in Signal dugout all men were employed on front line support trench R2 by night. By day work carried on as for the 1st.	
	5.		All work exactly as for 4th.	

Army Form C. 2118

WAR DIARY
or
INTELLIGENCE SUMMARY
(Erase heading not required.)

Sheet. 2.

Place	Date	Hour	Summary of Events and Information	Remarks and references to Appendices
Ypres- (St Eloi.) and REST AREA. (Moneuse)	February 1916. 6.		Back Sections Parties were employed in clearing wagons and preparing to move into REST AREA.	J.Army Corps No 1
			Forward Sections By night a party worked with the 13th Kings on front line support trench R₂. By day parties worked on BROOKE AVENUE C.T., the Dressing Station, IX Corps Signal dugout, dugouts in SCOTTISH WOOD, in the "P" trenches and the entrance to bombing post in R₃.	
	7.		Back Sections cleaned up billets. A billetting party of 1 Officer and 6 men moved to rest area by train. The Mounted section started for rest area by road and for the night at ZERMEZEELE.	
			Forward Section parties worked in R₃ and dugouts in SCOTTISH WOOD; also on drainage and cleaning of billets. During the evening the Section were relieved by the 93rd. Field Coy. (forward section ?)	
	8.		The Mounted Section proceeded by road from ZERMEZEELE to the new billets in rest area. The dismounted section marched by road to GODEWAERSVELDTE, and by train to St. OMER from there by road to new billets. The Back billets were handed over to the 93rd Coy. Field Cory R.E., and one Officer was left behind to assist the relieving unit.	
	9.		The Company unpacked transport and did necessary fatigues at new billets.	

WAR DIARY
or
INTELLIGENCE SUMMARY

(Erase heading not required.)

Army Form C. 2118

Sheet 3

Instructions regarding War Diaries and Intelligence Summaries are contained in F.S. Regs., Part II. and the Staff Manual respectively. Title Pages will be prepared in manuscript.

Place	Date	Hour	Summary of Events and Information	Remarks and references to Appendices
Les Oies. MONTECOVE	February 1916			
	10.		The Company carried out physical drill before breakfast. Three Sections marched to HOULLE for bridging practice. One Section employed on fatigues in Billets.	
	11.		Training and work as for 10.t. but two men worked on baths at BAYENGHEM.	
	12.			
	13. (Sunday)		Beyond necessary fatigues no work was done.	
	14.		Training work as for 10.t. but two men employed at the Divisional Cinema — BAYENGHEM.	
	15.			
	16.		Training work as for 10.t. but the Section at bridging were brought back at 12.30 p.m. as "stand bye" orders had been received from 8.c Brigade. During afternoon a party removed a tree which had fallen across the CHATEAU CONCOVE ROAD.	
	17th		The Coy paraded for physical drill before breakfast. In the morning Squad & Section drill was carried out & company drill in the afternoon — Mounted section — haunts inspection in the afternoon.	
	18th to 19th		Parade before breakfast — physical drill. Morning parade — route march. Afternoon parade Coy drill. Parties were sent to BAYENGHEM & NOTRE DAME for work on baths. A party was also employed making a "french stop" for & in flooding C.T.3 when needed.	

Army Form C. 2118
Sheet 4.

WAR DIARY
or
INTELLIGENCE SUMMARY
(Erase heading not required.)

Instructions regarding War Diaries and Intelligence Summaries are contained in F.S. Regs., Part II. and the Staff Manual respectively. Title Pages will be prepared in manuscript.

Place	Date	Hour	Summary of Events and Information	Remarks and references to Appendices
MONNECOVE — REST AREA —	February 1916 20th		To-day being Sunday, there were no parades except for bathing. A small party worked on the "French stop".	
	21st		Parade before breakfast – Physical drill. Morning + afternoon parades – Musketry. Also Section + Extended order drill.	
	22nd		Early parade – Physical drill. One section was sent to SALPERWICK to bring back pontooning equipment. One section was employed on fatigues + making targets + the "french stop". A party was sent in the afternoon with motor lorries to fetch timber from STONER. Remainder continued with squad + section drill + musketry.	
	23rd		Training + work – same as for 22nd except that no party was sent to STONER but Carpenters were employed at the Cinema Hall at BAYENGHEM.	
	24th		Training + work – same as for 23rd. 1 officer + 3 N.C.Os reported to operation branch G.H.Q.	
	25th		Training – same as for 24th. A party went to STONER to fetch timber. 2 N.C.Os were sent to 8th Field Amblce. to undergo a course of instruction in protection against gas.	
	26th		Early parade – Physical drill. A small scheme was carried out this morning, the general idea being that a convoy was trying to get through to WATTEN. Three sections being sent to intercept it. The convoy consisted of 26 men + were inoculated to-day.	

J. [signature] Major

Army Form C. 2118

WAR DIARY
or
INTELLIGENCE SUMMARY

Sheet 5.

(Erase heading not required.)

Place	Date	Hour	Summary of Events and Information	Remarks and references to Appendices
MONNEGUVE REST AREA —	February 1916 27th		Church parade 10.15 a.m. Small parties were sent to the baths at BAYENGHEM during the morning.	Bayenghem Maps
	28th		Early parade – Physical drill – Morning parades – Infantry & Section drill & musketry instruction. Another party of 26 NCOs men were inoculated to-day 1 Officer & 4 O.R. were sent for a course at the Divl. Grenade school.	
	29th		Training – same as for 28th.	

3rd Divisional Engineers.

1/1st CHESHIRE FIELD COMPANY R.E.

MARCH 1 9 1 6.

Army Form C. 2118

WAR DIARY
or
INTELLIGENCE SUMMARY

Sheet 1.

(Erase heading not required.)

Instructions regarding War Diaries and Intelligence Summaries are contained in F.S. Regs., Part II. and the Staff Manual respectively. Title Pages will be prepared in manuscript.

Place	Date	Hour	Summary of Events and Information	Remarks and references to Appendices
REST AREA. MONNE COVE.	March 1916 1st.		The whole Coy. paraded before breakfast for physical drill. During the morning one section carried out rapid firing instruction on the range. The remainder did Coy. drill and a route march. In the afternoon lectures was given to the men on protective measures against gas attacks. Working parties were also employed on shower baths at NOTRE DAME. Tub machine gun emplacement and full gun loop hole.	J. Waynes Maj 9.
	2nd.		Routine & work same as for 1st. except sections not on "Outpost Scheme".	
	3rd.		Work and instruction same as for 2nd. except that no further lectures were given.	
	4th.		Routine and work as for the 1st. The mounted section also being given musketry instruction on the range.	
	5th.		The whole Coy paraded at 6am to March △ Tre. road up wagons preparatory to moving from REST AREA. The Mounted Section marched out at 10 a.m. proceeding to new area by road. The Smoke helmets of the remainder of Company were inspected.	
	6th.		The Coy paraded at 11 am and marched to St. OMER when Key entrained for new area at OUDERDOM arriving there about 1.30 am on the 7th.	
YPRES- (The BLUFF.)	7th.		During morning all men were employed on necessary fatigues. In the afternoon two sections proceeded to forward billets in the CANAL BANK. (YPRES. COMMINES CANAL.) near The BLUFF.	
	8th.		Back Section. Employed on fatigues in billets. Forward Section. The cleaning & drainage of PEAR TREE WALK. This work was carried on with assistance of Pioneers by day worked on by night.	

1875 Wt. W593/826 1,000,000 4/15 J.B.C. & A. A.D.S.S./Forms/C. 2118.

Army Form C. 2118

WAR DIARY or INTELLIGENCE SUMMARY

(Erase heading not required.)

Sheet 2.

Instructions regarding War Diaries and Intelligence Summaries are contained in F.S. Regs., Part II. and the Staff Manual respectively. Title Pages will be prepared in manuscript.

Place	Date	Hour	Summary of Events and Information	Remarks and references to Appendices
YPRES – (St ELOI) The BLUFF	March 1916 9th		<u>Back Section</u> These worked on additional hut and air fatigue. <u>Forward Section</u> By night and day parties assisted by 6th S.W.B. Pioneer Batn. continued with the draining and cleaning of PEAR TREE WALK C.T. Small parties also were employed in laying trench boards from CANAL BANK to the C.T. and doing repairs to railway.	Murphy Major
	10th		Work as for 9th but in addition a party started draining the BLUFF C.T.	
	11th		Work as for 9th. After completion of night work both Sections less 1 NCO & 2 Sappers who remained in charge of dugouts and stores, marched out to Back Billets. The following day work was carried on by East Riding Coy R.E. who took over stores and billets.	Billets of EAST RIDING Coy R.E.
	12th		The Coy which had been occupying temporarily the Convent School VOORMEZEELE moved over to old billet across road at G.36.A.74. Two Sections moved out to new forward billets in building up parapet of Support Line trench Q2.	
	13th		<u>Back Section</u> were employed on wire entanglement near killer. Found Sections continued by night work on Q2 and draining of QUEEN VICTORIA ST.	
	14th		<u>Back Section</u> Parties worked at Brigade Hd Qrs, on Dugouts, on Torpedoes at Billets, and at Hutting Dump. Forward Section work as for 13th.	
	15th		<u>Back Section</u> Parties prepared material for forward work and other work carried on as for 14th. <u>Forward Section</u> work as for 13th and in addition the laying of Trench Boards in Support Line R7 was commenced.	

WAR DIARY
or
INTELLIGENCE SUMMARY Sheet 3.

Army Form C. 2118

Place	Date	Hour	Summary of Events and Information	Remarks and references to Appendices
YPRES - (St. ELOI)	March 1916. 16th		Back Section - Two men were employed at trotting dump. Remainder on fatigues etc. at Gillet. Forward Sections (three). A party, assisted by party of 13th King's continued work on drainage of Queen Victoria St. C.T. A party, assisted by party of Queen Victoria St. C.T. continued laying trench boards in R7. One section commenced building new trench dugouts near Convent Lane C.T. All remaining were continued work of rebuilding parapet of Q2 trench.	Heavy gas on Hats.
	17th		Back Section - Work as for 16th. Forward Sections - Party continued laying trench boards in R7. Party assisted by party of 50 E. Yorks to fill sandbags worked on parapet of R5. One section continued work on new trench dugouts. Small party repaired tramline between VOORMEZEELE & DICKEBUSCH. Remainder assisted by parties of infantry continued work on Q2.	
	18th & 19th		Back Section - Work as for 17th. Forward Sections - 1 Section continued work on new trench dug-outs. 2 Sections (assisted by infantry parties) worked on building up the parapet of Q2. CELLAR LANE C.T. & MOUND LANE C.T. 1 Man wounded tonight.	
	19th		Back Section - Work as for 18th. Forward Sections - 1 section continued work on trench dugouts. A small party repaired pumps in VOORMEZEELE. A small party repaired railway between DICKEBUSCH & VOORMEZEELE. Remainder continued work on Q2. 1 Man wounded tonight.	
	20th		Work for Back + forward sections same as for 19th.	
	21st		Back Section - Work as for 20th. Forward Sections - One section continued work on new trench dugouts. A party worked on pumps in VOORMEZEELE. Remainder worked on parapet of Q2 & repairing trench boards in MOUND LANE C.T. 1 Man wounded.	
	22nd		Back Section - Work as for 21st. Forward Sections - One section continued work on trench dugouts. A party repaired tramline between DICKEBUSCH & VOORMEZEELE. A party worked by day on strutting of WHITE HORSE CELLARS. Remainder worked on Q2.	

WAR DIARY
INTELLIGENCE SUMMARY
Sheet 4.

Army Form C. 2118

Place	Date	Hour	Summary of Events and Information	Remarks and references to Appendices
/PRES. (St Eloi.)	March 1916 23rd		Back Section work as for 16th. Forward Section. By day a party of Killed WHITE HORSE CELLARS. By night work same as for 22nd. also a party assisted by small number of Infantry cleared CELLAR LANE C.T. During evening R. Butler were shelled and two men wounded —	J. Boyle Simon Major.
	24.		Back and Forward Sections work as per 23rd.	
	25.		Back Section. Work as for 16th. Forward Section. Work on dugouts continued and repairs made to gaps in front support trenches caused by shell fire.	
	26.		The Back Section moved up to DICKEBUSCH. Forward Section. A party supervised carrying up of material to forward R.E. dumps. A small party assisted by day the blowing standing of Brigade Ld. Ok. The Section in enemy moved back to DICKEBUSCH.	
	27.		Lieut. T. CHALLONER with three NCOs and men went forward with attacking party to reconnoitre ground between and behind the Mine Craters, blown up at 4.15am preceding attack on enemy's trenches. The Company moved up at dusk and worked on repairs and leaving of CELLAR LANE C.T. and R2. Little work was possible owing to the very severe shelling. Later the Coy. had orders to stand to for enemy Counter attack. During course of night work three Officers. Captain J. Williams. Lieut. G.F.Watson D.S.O. and Lieut. C.H. Kingman and 7 N.C.Os and Men were wounded — (One Officer since died from wounds.)	

Army Form C. 2118

WAR DIARY
or
INTELLIGENCE SUMMARY
(Erase heading not required.)

Sheet 5.

Instructions regarding War Diaries and Intelligence Summaries are contained in F. S. Regs., Part II. and the Staff Manual respectively. Title Pages will be prepared in manuscript.

Place	Date	Hour	Summary of Events and Information	Remarks and references to Appendices
YPRES (S. E. 10/)	March 1916 28th		The whole Coy. came back to billets at OUDERDOM during afternoon — Lieut. C.H. Kinsman died from wounds received on previous day. —	Reginald Power Major
	29th		Two Sections moved up to VOORMEZEELE at 5.30pm and working parties were sent up to the support lines but were heavily shelled and little work was possible. The men returning at 2 am. — The following NCOs received cards in respect of having been Mentioned in Despatches :— 4. C.S.M. Armstrong J. 233 C.Q.M.S. Conway J. 524 Corp. Allan S.B. 700 " " Macleod. A. 104 " " Vick J.	
	30th		Two Sections worked on clearing opening out old front line trenches Pub. Duncan Lane and Q.A. —	
	31st		The two back Sections moved up to DICKEBUSCH. The whole Coy. worked in drainage of new front line, i.e. Captured trenches — during course of work the enemy attempted a Counter attack and all men were helped to reinforce front line. The attack did not extend to this sector and after Signallers was received the Company was ordered to withdraw and returned to Billets. No Casualties. —	

3rd Divisional Engineers.

1/1st CHESHIRE FIELD COMPANY R.E.

APRIL 1916.

WAR DIARY 1/1 Cheshire Field Company R.E.

Army Form C.2118
Vol 15

INTELLIGENCE SUMMARY.
(Erase heading not required.)

Place	Date	Hour	Summary of Events and Information	Remarks and references to Appendices
			April 1916	
ST ELOI	1st 2nd 3rd 4th		The whole company was employed draining & clearing new trenches at St Eloi – working in parties by day & night	
	5th		The company returned to rear billets in the early morning & the day was employed in loading transport ready for moving	
MONT DES CATS	6th to 18th		The Company moved into Rest Area. The Company were on Rest. Time was spent in Company training, overhauling of Tools, Wagons & experiments on Demolitions	
	19th 20		The Company moved from Rest Area to New position. All available men were employed on Vierstraat Switch together with four companies of R.W.F. & 300 men of 1st Entrenching Battalion on digging, repairing & revetting reserve line & barbed wire entanglements.	Regulars Maj.
VIERSTRAAT	21st		do with 400 men of 1st Gordons & 300 of 1st Entrenching Battalion. Swinging platers at DICKEBUSCH lake. over.	

WAR DIARY
or
INTELLIGENCE SUMMARY

Army Form C. 2118.

Sheet 2

Cheshire Field Company R.E.

Place	Date	Hour	Summary of Events and Information	Remarks and references to Appendices
	22nd		April continued	Hampson Major
			All available men employed on the VIERSTRAAT switch with 400 men of 1st Gordons + 300 of No 1 Entrenching Battalion. Good progress was made on wiring + supporting points. R.E. Dump at MITRE KRUIS taken over	
	23rd to 30th		No 3 section proceeded to Advanced Billets. Two forward sections employed each night with assistance of 300 infantry men in reconstructing New Support Line between M + N trenches, laying duckboards in BOIS CARRÉ C.T., repairing + installing tram line, gaps in CHICORY C.T. + P + O C.T. also drawing front line M trenches + digging new C.T. to Reserve line.	
			Awards: Lieut T Mallon was awarded the Military Cross on the 24th	
			Casualties:- 2 Sappers Wounded 28/4/16 29/4/16	
			1. T. J. O Dawson Wounded at VIERSTRAAT on the 25/4/16	

3rd Divisional Engineers.

1/1ST CHESHIRE FIELD COMPANY R.E.

MAY 1916.

WAR DIARY
or
INTELLIGENCE SUMMARY

Army Form C. 2118
SHEET 1.

Place	Date	Hour	Summary of Events and Information	Remarks and references to Appendices
VIERSTRAAT AREA.	MAY 1916 1st to 26th		During this period the work of the Company was of an ordered nature only altering in small details from day to day. Two Sections were quartered at forward billets and carried on all night work except PONNY LANE C.T. which was done by one of the Sections brought down nightly from Back Billets. The remaining Section was employed on day work and prepared material for night parties. The chief items of work were as follows:— Construction of Support Line in rear of front line M and N trenches. Putting BOIS CARRÉ C.T. in repair including the revetting of same with trench frames, laying duckboards, and building parapet parados. Building parados of H1 Support Line & strengthening of existing work. Construction of new Communication trench (part of POPPY LANE) to Reserve Line near VIERSTRAAT. A patrol of the front line and main road was made and damage caused by shell fire repaired nightly. In addition to the main work as necessity arose parties were sent to repair damage in C.T.'s and Redoubts caused by gun fire during the day. All the above was night work. The day work covered sundry small jobs carried out at different times during the month amongst which was the construction of a strong wooden framed dugout at HALLEBAST — a Bomb Store in RIDGEWOOD. Repair of dam at KEMMEL WATER Supply. Laying of new water pipe line to RIDGEWOOD. Repair of pumps at DURHAM HUTS. Repair of machine gun emplacement in front line. From the 16th we had 1 N.C.O. detailed with party of D.A.C. started preparation of work on strong brick O.P.'s for the R.F.A. in VIERSTRAAT neighbourhood. We had also 1 N.C.O. attached to T.M. Battery to assist in emplacements. One sapper running pumping station.	Jasper Page Major

Army Form C. 2118.

1/1 Cheshire f.Coy
Sheet 2.
R.E.

WAR DIARY
or
INTELLIGENCE SUMMARY.
(Erase heading not required.)

Place	Date	Hour	Summary of Events and Information	Remarks and references to Appendices
VIERSTRAAT AREA.	May 1916			
	1st to 26th	Continued.	During this time night working parties often came under shell and machine gun fire but fortunately for the Coy. only three Sappers were wounded though the infantry parties had a number of casualties especially on the "M and N" support line mostly caused by high explosive.	Appendices Nos.
	27.		The Company was relieved by the 7th Field Coy R.E. and marched out at 4.30 pm for REST AREA which was reached at 4.30 pm the march being done in good time nothing of event taking place.	
	28.		Sunday. An inspection of all equipment & accoutrements was made during the morning. No further work done.	Appendices Nos.
Rest Area.	29th to 31st		Company training was carried out. {struck out} Section Drill. 6.30 – 7.30 am Company Drill & Rifle exercises from 9 to 10.30 am. Route march in full marching order 11 am to 2 pm. Afternoon no work done.	

3rd Divisional Engineers.

1/1ST CHESHIRE FIELD COMPANY R.E.

JUNE 1916.

WAR DIARY or INTELLIGENCE SUMMARY

Army Form C. 2118

1/1 Cheshire Field Coy R.E.   Sheet 1.   Vol 17

Place	Date	Hour	Summary of Events and Information	Remarks and references to Appendices
REST AREA MONT de CAT	June 1916 1st		The Company was preparing for an inspection by the C.R.E. when it got orders to move up in six hours. The Coy. marched out to LACLYTTE at 8 p.m. where it arrived at temporary billets at 10.35 p.m.	
	2nd		The Coy. moved to billets at SHERPENBERG, where some of the men being accommodated in bivouacs which we erected. Work on O.Ps for 1st R.F.A. was taken over from the 2nd Field Coy R.E. and proceeded with.	
SHERPENBERG	3rd		Work by day was continued on the Bride Town O.Ps. The following names were gazetted and honours received:– Major Wayne Morgan (O.C. Company) – Military Cross. No. 4. Sergt. Jarmaston J. D.C.M. – Previously mentioned Russian in dispatches. " 700. A/Corpl. Macleod. A. Military Medal " 524 " Allan. G.B. " " 104 " Vick. J. " "	J. Wayne Morgan Major
	4.		The work on the Bride Tower O.Ps was continued by day. One N.C.O. being wounded & in course of 7 days work. Orders to be prepared to move in four hours were received. Work on the O.Ps was commenced by night. A Church parade was held during the morning.	
	5.		Work on O.Ps by day and night was continued with the whole Company being employed and assisted by gunners from the D.A.C.	
	6. to 15.		During this period work was carried on by day and night on O.Ps without interruption except on the 11th. A Church parade was held for the few men not out on work and divisions.	
	16.		Work by day as usual. No parties sent out at night as marching orders had been received. Very heavy gunning was heard on our front also to west of the fire from 11 p.m. and continued for several hours. No train "Stando" was received however.	
	17.		All transport packed in early morning and Coy. marched out at 8 a.m. for FLETRE where it billeted for the night. March done in good time and no casualties.	
	18.		The Coy. paraded at 8 a.m. and joined up with the detail from 3rd Division.	

WAR DIARY or INTELLIGENCE SUMMARY

CHESHIRE FIELD Coy. RE   Army Form C. 2118.   Sheet 2.

Place	Date	Hour	Summary of Events and Information	Remarks and references to Appendices
	June 1916.			
OSTERZEELE	18.		at 9 am the Coy. proceeding to OSTERZEELE where it was billeted for the night. A foot inspection was made and was found to be in very good order.	
ISERZEELE	19.		The Coy. paraded at 8.15 am and marched to LEDERZEELE, a foot inspection showing few cases requiring attention. The Coy. was billeted for the night in the village.	
LEULINGHEM	20.		The Coy. turned up into the Column at 9 am and marched to LEULINGHEM village which was reached at 2 p.m. No casualties. Foot inspection Satisfactory.	
"	21/st		The Coy. paraded at 6.30 am. Squad drill - 9.30 am. An inspection of pit and equipment was made. Section and manual drill carried out - 2.30 p.m. All foot cart, pontoon wagons and transport wagons cleaned.	
"	22nd		The Coy. paraded at 6.30. Squad drill - 9 am. Full marching order and carried out an advance across country in attack until under artillery fire returning to billets at 3.30 p.m. also all transport taken out across country.	
"	23rd		Parade and work as per 22nd. One NCO was badly injured during the night by falling.	
"	24.		Work and parade as per 23rd - Returning at 1 p.m. In afternoon a 9 hour field drill (new method) was carried out.	
"	25.		Company paraded at 9 am and proceeded to MOULLE in Motor Lorries for Pontoon exercises. The GOC presented ribbons (Military Cross) to Major J. Wayne Morgan (OC Company) Sergt Armstrong and Corpl Vick (Military Medals) just before work was started. Coy. returned to Billets at 7.30 p.m.	J Wayne Morgan Major
"	26.		Pontooning carried out as per 26th	
"	27.		The Coy. paraded at 6.30 for Squad drill - 9 am. Route march material on trestle wagon reorganised in accordance with new arrangements. During the afternoon the Coy. practiced bridging broken ground and trenches. The work being done in good time. The NCOs were lectured by the CO on their duties.	
"	28.		Work as per 27. A lecture on Explosives demolition was given in afternoon.	
"	29.		" " " 28. but inspection instead in Full Marching Order and Route march.	
"	30.		Squad drill at 6.30 am. The Coy. bridged two gullies with special arrangement of Bridging Material. Coy. arrived in late and no further work done in afternoon.	

3rd Divisional Engineers.

1/1ST CHESHIRE FIELD COMPANY R.E.

JULY 1916.

Army Form C. 2118.

WAR DIARY
or
INTELLIGENCE SUMMARY.
(Erase heading not required.)

Sheet N° 1

Place	Date	Hour	Summary of Events and Information	Remarks and references to Appendices
ST OMER Area			CHESHIRE FIELD CO RE	
	1/7/16		The W/2 Company, with transport went out for a route march from 8 am to 12 noon. Orders were received to move the following morning.	Jones
	2/7/16		The Company paraded at 3.15 am, and moved out of LEULINGHEM at 3.30 am, and marched to WIZERNES, where we entrained, and left at 7.50 am. The Company detrained at FIENVILLERS - CANDAS at 6 p.m, and marched to EPECAMPS where we billeted for the night, arriving at 11 p.m.	Jones
	3/7/16		Company paraded 9 am and joined 8 Infantry Brigade on line of march at 9.50 am and marched to MONTONVILLERS, which was reached at 1.30 p.m. We were billeted in the Chateau. Inspection of feet, kits, and equipment.	Jones
	4/7/16		Rested at MONTONVILLERS until 8.30 pm, when we moved out to join 8th Infantry Brigade on line of march at 9 p.m. We were billeted at CARDONETTE for the night, arriving there at 1.45 am.	Jones
	5/7/16		Rested at CARDONETTE, and only had usual foot, arms and gas helmet inspection. We paraded at 6.30 p.m and joined 8th Infantry Brigade on line of march and marched through CORBIE to VAUX CAMP, where we arrived at 3 a.m.	Jones
	6/7/16		Usual inspection in morning of feet, arms, and smoke helmets. Moved out of camp at 3 p.m and marched in dependently to BRAY, where we bivouaced for the night, arriving at 7.30 p.m.	Jones

Army Form C. 2118.

WAR DIARY
or
INTELLIGENCE SUMMARY.

(Erase heading not required.)

Sheet N° 2

Instructions regarding War Diaries and Intelligence Summaries are contained in F. S. Regs., Part II. and the Staff Manual respectively. Title pages will be prepared in manuscript.

Place	Date	Hour	Summary of Events and Information	Remarks and references to Appendices
			CHESHIRE FIELD CO RE	
	7/7/16		At 8 am N°s 1 & 2 Sections moved up to CARNOY to dugouts and relieved the 79th Field Co RE of Div. N° 3 Section moved up to CARNOY at 2 pm. N° 4 Section was kept at BRAY to make entire boards and other fatigue work. N°s 1, 2, & 3 Sections worked on the BLIND ALLEY communication trench in the evening. Transport lines remained at BRAY	✓
	8/7/16		The three forward Sections were employed (the whole day) forming dumps of RE material on the MONTAUBAN - CARNOY Road for 8th Brigade. 2/Lieuts M°GILL & SINCLAIR joined unit.	✓
	9/7/16		Work was continued on the dumps the whole day, and the Brigade started carrying. N° 4 Section went out in evening to deepen BLIND ALLEY, with a working party of 150 Royal Scots and to make bridge over trench. N° 3 Section went out to build bridge over trench, and a gas shell fell close to this party, and all the section felt the effects slightly, and one man suffered severely and was admitted to Hospital	(
	10/7/16		Carrying parties and transport were employed in forming advance dumps during the day. Two Sections went out in the evening to work on BLIND ALLEY with 150 Royal Scots. Orders were received at 10.50 p.m. to destroy German Field guns in CATERPILLAR VALLEY. When IC party reached CATERPILLAR VALLEY, four 4.2 Howitzers were found, one with the barrel off. The charges were laid on three guns, but the detonators failed, and the guns were not destroyed.	✓

Army Form C. 2118.

Sheet No 2

WAR DIARY
or
INTELLIGENCE SUMMARY.
(Erase heading not required.)

Place	Date	Hour	Summary of Events and Information	Remarks and references to Appendices
			CHESHIRE FIELD Co R E	
	11/7/16		Lt ROBERTSHAW took out No 2 Section to dig a bridge over BLIND ALLEY and to deepen BLIND ALLEY communication trench. He was assisted by a party of infantry. At 8.15 pm the CRE gave orders for two strong points to be constructed on the North side of CATERPILLAR VALLEY. The C.R.E, Major MORGAN, and Capt. HOLDEN went on to site the positions for these strong points. IInd Lieut WARD was to bring on Section No 1, 3 & 4 with material. Owing to the congestion of traffic on the tracks and in the trenches the party did not arrive in CATERPILLAR VALLEY until 1.45 a.m., and it was then too late to start work. Our Sappers were employed carrying up material to dumps.	
	12/7/16		Transport and carrying parties were employed during the day in taking material up to the dumps. The four sections went out in the evening to construct the two strong points in CATERPILLAR VALLEY, and worked until 2.15 p.m., when the work was completed.	
	13/7/16		The sections were in billets all day. The transport was employed in taking material up to the dumps. In the evening No 1 Section under IInd Lieut McGILL moved off to join the 9th Brigade, and No 3 Section under IInd Lieut WARD to join the 8th Brigade, to take part in the operations ordered for the 14/7/16.	

Army Form C. 2118.

Sheet No 4

WAR DIARY
or
INTELLIGENCE SUMMARY.
(Erase heading not required.)

Place	Date	Hour	Summary of Events and Information	Remarks and references to Appendices
	14/7/16		CHESHIRE FIELD CO. R.E. The III Div. attacked the enemy's Second Line from BAZANTIN-LE-GRAND to LONGUEVAL. The attack took place at 3.25 a.m, having been preceded by a very heavy bombardment. Nos 2 & 4 Sections were ordered up to make bridges for horse transport and field artillery over MONTAUBAN ALLEY, and two bridges were erected. The transport was employed in bringing up material to the dumps, and in the evening sandbags were worked up to the dumps and CATERPILLAR VALLEY for the 9th Brigade. No 3 Section went forward with the 8th Brigade in the attack was held up in front of the German line up their wire and cutting heavy casualties. Lieut. C.R. WARD and 3 O.R. killed and 15 O.R. wounded.	
	15/7/16		Two sections were sent up to cut the wire in front of the enemy old trenches, and in the evening two sections went up to assist the 2nd ROYAL SCOTS in making strong points near LONGUEVAL. Two O.R. wounded	
	16/7/16		As heavy guns and motor lorries were being taken over the bridges erected over MONTAUBAN ALLEY for horse transport and field guns, two sections were ordered up to build a bridge capable of carrying 15 Tons, and this was completed by 9.30 p.m. Two sections went up to assist the 2nd ROYAL SCOTS in completing strong points, but were relieved & return by O.C. 2nd ROYAL SCOTS.	

T/134. Wt. W708-776. 500000. 4/15. Sir J. C. & S.

Army Form C. 2118.

WAR DIARY
or
INTELLIGENCE SUMMARY.
(Erase heading not required.)

Sheet N°25

Place	Date	Hour	Summary of Events and Information	Remarks and references to Appendices
			CHESHIRE FIELD Co. R.E.	
	17/7/16		A small party was sent up to keep the bridges over MONTAUBAN ALLEY clean, and to improve the approaches to same. N° 2 Section went out to improve the bridges over BLIND ALLEY, and on returning, N° ROBERTSHAW who was in charge of the section reported, that a tremendous number of small shells, which only made a very slight noise when they burst, had been falling near them. These must have been the German new type of gas shell. The section suffered no casualties through the shells. Two sections were ordered by the 8th Brigade to assist the 8th ROYAL SCOTS on strong points during the night, but these orders were cancelled.	[signature]
	18/7/16		A small party was kept on the bridges over MONTAUBAN ALLEY. Two sections were sent out to make a new deep wealther fork and improve the old works to CATERPILLAR VALLEY.	[signature]
	19/7/16		Received orders to keep the company standing by, and await orders from 8th Infantry Brigade. Transport worked up material to dump, and also shovels and pickets for the 8th Brigade.	[signature]
	20/7/16		Again ordered to stand by and await orders from 8th Infantry Brigade. Transport was working material up to dumps.	[signature]
	21/7/16		Standing by to await orders from 8th Brigade. Transport employed in taking material up to dumps	[signature]
	22/7/16		As the 8th Brigade did not require the sections for any particular work, the whole company were sent out to work on repairs to CARNOY to MONTAUBAN ROAD.	[signature]
			Casualties. 1 O.R. wounded.	

Army Form C. 2118.

WAR DIARY
or
INTELLIGENCE SUMMARY.
(Erase heading not required.)

Sheet N° 6

Instructions regarding War Diaries and Intelligence Summaries are contained in F. S. Regs., Part II. and the Staff Manual respectively. Title pages will be prepared in manuscript.

CHESHIRE FIELD CO. R.E.

Place	Date	Hour	Summary of Events and Information	Remarks and references to Appendices
	23/7/16		The 8th Brigade did not require any assistance, so the company were ordered to parade "to repair" to the CARNOY to MONTAUBAN Road. As the company was about to move off, orders were received from C.R.E. to recall all working parties. Orders to work on French gun North end of TRONES WOOD which had been started and which ran in a N.W. direction. The company paraded for this work at 8 p.m. and were met on site by 200 men of 2nd SUFFOLKS, and worked until 2.15 a.m. Casualties Lieut CHALLONER wounded. 1 O.R. Killed and 8 O.R. wounded, two of whom returned to duty.	
	24/7/16		Received orders to report to 8th Brigade, and received orders from them to make three strong points after 1st infantry had assaulted and taken a trench near WATERLOT FARM, on the morning of 25/7/16. These orders were cancelled at 5.15 p.m. Received orders from C.R.E. to clear LONGUEVAL ALLEY. Company marched out at 8 p.m. for this work. There was a big bombardment soon after the company had started out, and it was found that all troops to trenches on the way up to LONGUEVAL ALLEY were standing to, and later there was an alarm of a gas attack. Every effort was made to get to the work, but the company eventually had to return, and arrived back at billets at 2.15 a.m. Casualties 1 O.R. wounded (self inflicted)	

Army Form C. 2118.

Sheet No 7

WAR DIARY
or
INTELLIGENCE SUMMARY.
(Erase heading not required.)

Instructions regarding War Diaries and Intelligence Summaries are contained in F. S. Regs., Part II. and the Staff Manual respectively. Title pages will be prepared in manuscript.

Place	Date	Hour	Summary of Events and Information	Remarks and references to Appendices
			CHESHIRE FIELD Co. R.E.	
	25/7/16		At 9.30 am orders were received that the Division was to be relieved by the II Division. This unit was relieved by the 226th Field Co. R.E. and marched out of CARNOY at 2 pm, and proceeded to HAPPY VALLEY, where the transport from back billets joined the unit. The company bivouaced for the night in HAPPY VALLEY.	
	26/7/16		The company paraded in the morning for section drill. Orders were received from the 8th Brigade that 'a' company was to march to MAULTE leaving HAPPY VALLEY at 4.45 pm. The company marched to MAULTE and went into billets there. II Lieuts THOMPSON, GOURLEY and COTTLE joined the unit from England, and a draft of 15 O.R. also joined from the Base.	
	27/7/16		In the morning the billets, which were in a very filthy condition when we arrived, were cleaned, and afterwards the company paraded for squad and section drill. At the request of the 8th Brigade a stage was erected for the performance given in the evening by the MUDLARKS. The company paraded for a bathing parade in the afternoon.	
	28/7/16		In the morning the company paraded for kit inspection and afterwards for squad and section drill. In the afternoon the whole of the transport was cleaned and the tool carts overhauled.	
	29/7/16		The company paraded for squad and section drill and afterwards went for a route march. Bathing parade in the afternoon.	

Army Form C. 2118.

Sheet N° 5

WAR DIARY
or
INTELLIGENCE SUMMARY.
(Erase heading not required.)

Place	Date	Hour	Summary of Events and Information	Remarks and references to Appendices
			CHESHIRE FIELD CO. R.E.	
	30/7/16		Orders were received that the company was to move to WELLCOME WOOD and to pull down huts there, this work to start on Aug 1st, and also to remove a bell tower from near CHIPILLY to MEAULTE. Officers were sent to reconnoitre the roads and see the work. In the morning the Company paraded with the 8th EAST YORKS for Divine Service. In the afternoon there was a tug-of-war competition between two teams from the 8th EAST YORKS and two teams from this unit. In both cases the teams from the EAST YORKS were beaten.	
	31/7/16		The company marched out from MEAULTE at 11 a.m., the band of the 8th EAST YORKS playing us out of the village. One section proceeded to the site of the bell tower near CHIPILLY and bivouaced there, the remainder of the company proceeded to WELLCOME WOOD and billetted in the huts there.	

Joseph Andrews Major.
O.C. Cheshire Field Co. R.E.

3rd Divisional Engineers

1/1st CHESHIRE FIELD COMPANY R. E.

AUGUST 1916

WAR DIARY
or
INTELLIGENCE SUMMARY.
(Erase heading not required.)

Army Form C. 2118.

1/1 Cheshire Fd Coy R.E.

Sheet No 1.

Place	Date	Hour	Summary of Events and Information	Remarks and references to Appendices
			CHESHIRE FIELD COY. R.E.	
	1/8/16		The three sections in WELLCOME WOOD started to pull down its huts. The Section near CHIPILLY worked on dismantling its bath house. The C.E. XIII Corps was seen at ETINEHEM, and arranged for huts Lorries to be detailed for the 2nd inst. to remove huts to the CITADEL and the bath house to MEAULTE. It was arranged that an officer should meet the C.E. XIII Corps at the CITADEL on the morning of the 2nd in order that the exact site for the huts should be allotted.	
	2/9/16		2nd Lieut. THOMPSON and No. 3 Section moved up to the CITADEL VALLEY on the four Lorries which arrived at WELLCOME WOOD to remove huts. 2nd Lieut. THOMPSON met the C.E. XIII Corps at the CITADEL and was shown the site to start the erection of huts on. Each Lorry did two trips, and eight huts were transported. 2nd Lieut McGILL having dismantled the bath house, and having transported its material, except the engine and boiler to MEAULTE, moved his section to MEAULTE in the evening, leaving a guard of CHIPILLY to pull down its huts in WELLCOME WOOD. Arrangements were made with the 232 Army Troops Co. to borrow lifting tackle to move the boiler.	
	3/9/16		The two sections in WELLCOME WOOD continued to dismantle huts, and the section at the CITADEL continued erecting the huts. Four Lorries were employed in transporting huts and each made three trips, taking altogether twelve huts. The section at MEAULTE worked on re-erecting the bath house. Tackle for lifting the boiler was obtained from the 232 Army Troops Co., but the C.E. XIII Corps used to say he would not obtain a suitable lorry until the 5th inst.	

T/2131. Wt. W708-776. 500000. 4/15. Sir J. C. & S.

Army Form C. 2118.

WAR DIARY
or
INTELLIGENCE SUMMARY.
(Erase heading not required.)

Instructions regarding War Diaries and Intelligence Summaries are contained in F. S. Regs., Part II. and the Staff Manual respectively. Title pages will be prepared in manuscript.

Sheet N° 2.

CHESHIRE FIELD COY, R.E.

Place	Date	Hour	Summary of Events and Information	Remarks and references to Appendices
	4/8/16		Two sections continued to dismantle huts in WELLCOME WOOD. One section continued to work on the erection of huts at the CITADEL and the other section worked on re-erecting bath house at MEAULTE. Information was received from A.S.C. that they were sending a special lorry to CHIPILLY to remove boils on morning of 5ᵗʰ, so a party was sent from WELLCOME WOOD in the afternoon to rig up the lifting tackle. Four lorries were removing huts from WELLCOME WOOD to the CITADEL but only six huts were removed, as the springs on two lorries broke on the first trip.	
	5/8/16		A party was sent down from WELLCOME WOOD to CHIPILLY in the morning to load up boilers, and same was then taken over to MEAULTE. Work was continued dismantling huts in WELLCOME WOOD, erecting huts at CITADEL and erecting bath house at MEAULTE. No huts were removed today.	
	6/8/16		Four lorries arrived in the morning to remove huts from WELLCOME WOOD to the CITADEL, and N°2 Section under 2ⁿᵈ Lieut COTTLE went up on the first trip to assist N°3 Section in the erecting of the huts. Twelve huts were removed. N°1 Section continued to work on bath house at MEAULTE and N°4 Section was dismantling huts in WELLCOME WOOD	

Army Form C. 2118.

WAR DIARY
or
INTELLIGENCE SUMMARY.
(Erase heading not required.)

Sheet No 3.

Place	Date	Hour	Summary of Events and Information	Remarks and references to Appendices
			CHESHIRE FIELD COY. R.E.	
	7/8/16		Four Coivies arrived at WELLCOME WOOD in the morning and transported huts to the CITADEL. Work was carried on by No 4 dismantling huts at WELLCOME WOOD, Section No 2 03 erecting huts at the CITADEL, and No 1 Section erecting batt houses at MEAULTE. The four Coivies made three trips each, removing 16 huts.	✓
	8/8/16		Work was continued dismantling huts in WELLCOME WOOD, erecting huts at the CITADEL and erecting its batt houses at MEAULTE.	✓
	9/8/16		Work continued as on 8/8/16. Four Coivies were used for transporting huts from WELLCOME WOOD to the CITADEL, and 11 huts were removed.	✓
	10/8/16		Work was carried on at WELLCOME WOOD pulling down huts and clearing wood, at MEAULTE erecting batt houses, and at the CITADEL erecting huts. Orders were received from CE XIV Corps to remove batt houses from CHIPILLY WHARF to CARNOY, and an officer was sent to reconnoitre.	✓
	11/8/16		Orders arrived from C.R.E. at 2 a.m. to concentrate the company at the CITADEL and to take over work from EAST RIDING FIELD Co R.E. The portion of the company at WELLCOME WOOD marched at 11 a.m. and reached the CITADEL at 3 p.m. The section from MEAULTE arrived at the CITADEL at 1.30 p.m. Handed over our work to the 2/2nd WEST LANCS Co R.E. Officers went round with officers of EAST RIDING FIELD Co to reconnoitre the new areas since known as C & D near MONTAUBAN and the BRIQUETERIE. 2 Lieut BRADDOCK joined the unit from England.	✓

Army Form C. 2118.

WAR DIARY
or
INTELLIGENCE SUMMARY.
(Erase heading not required.)

CHESHIRE FIELD COY. R.E.

Sheet No. A

Place	Date	Hour	Summary of Events and Information	Remarks and references to Appendices
	12/8/16		Sections Nos 1 & 2 under 2/Lieut's ROBERTSHAW and COTTLE went out at 2 a.m. to work on Tr. C Reserve Line, and had a working party of 400 men from the 8th Brigade Composite Battalion. Work was also continued by sappers and a party of few infantry on the entrances to the two deep dugouts in the SUNKEN Lane at A.Sd.6.0. (MONTAUBAN Trench Map 1/20000). The work on the entrance to these dugouts was carried on by four 6 hour reliefs. Sections Nos 3 & 4 under 2/Lieuts THOMPSON & COTTLE went out at 7 p.m. to continue Tr. C Reserve Line, with 400 infantry from the 8th Brigade Composite Battalion.	
	13/8/16		As for the 12th as regards work. Capt HOLDEN was granted 5 days Special leave.	
	14/8/16		The work was continued by two sections and 400 infantry on Tr. C Reserve line, parties going out at 2 a.m. (Reciser) and to Mark 12 plan notice boards for use of 9th & 76th Brigades. These were made and delivered to Tr. STANLEY R.E. Dump. At 7 p.m. two sections and 400 men went out to work on the clearing of MALTZ HORN and CHIMPANZEE C.T.s. Three bridging wagons with material for the STANLEY DUMP were delivered up at 6 p.m. Casualties 1 O.R.	
	15/8/16		At 2 a.m. 2/Lieut BRADDOCK, 7 sappers and 36 men from the Composite Battalion of the 8th Infantry Brigade went out to work on the six dugouts started by the 2/1 WEST LANCS Co R.E. at A.Sd.3.A (MONTAUBAN Trench Map 1/20,000). At 8 a.m. 2/Lieut ROBERTSHAW took at the 2nd Relief, at 2 p.m. 2/Lieut McGILL the 3rd Relief, and 2/Lieut SINCLAIR the 4th Relief at 8 p.m. Three bridging wagons took material up to the STANLEY DUMP at 8 a.m. Work was stopped on the dugouts in the Sunken Road A.Sd.6.0 at 2 p.m.	

Army Form C. 2118.

WAR DIARY
or
INTELLIGENCE SUMMARY.
(Erase heading not required.)

SHEET No. 5.

CHESHIRE FIELD COY. R.E.

Place	Date	Hour	Summary of Events and Information	Remarks and references to Appendices
	15/8/16		Continued. In the afternoon four parties each comprising of 1 N.C.O and three sappers were sent to report to the 8th Brigade in order to work with special infantry parties in making of strong points.	
	16/8/16		Work was continued by 6 hour reliefs in the dugouts, as yesterday. Three wagon loads of material were sent up to the STANLEY DUMP at 5 am. Work in dugouts was stopped at 2 pm. Company was standing by ready to move at 15 minutes notice. Casualties 2.O.R.	
	17/8/16		The Company was standing by all day, ready to move at 15 minute notice. In the afternoon the C.R.E. called at billets and gave orders that the Company was to go out to clean JACKSON & MALTZ-HORN C.T.s at 3:30am tomorrow morning, if conditions were suitable.	
	18/8/16		The Company paraded at 3:30 am and marched off. 2nd Lieut McGILL had proceeded to C.R.E's Office at 3 am to get into touch with 9th Brigade. He was informed that owing to shelling going on, the Company could not work. He then met the Company and brought them back to billets, where they arrived at 4:50 am. Casualties 2.O.R.	
	19/8/16		The Company was stood out at 1:30 pm to clean MALTZ-HORN C.T. They worked 7:30 pm. when owing to a relief, they had to stop. Returned to billets at 9:30 pm. Casualties 7.O.R. including 2 slightly wounded and returned to duty.	

T/131. Wt. W708-776. 500000. 4/15. Sir J. C. & S.

WAR DIARY or INTELLIGENCE SUMMARY

CHESHIRE FIELD COY. R.E.

Sheet No 6.

Date	Hour	Summary of Events and Information	Remarks
20/8/16		Orders were received to move from the CITADEL to the SANDPITS with 8th Brigade Group. The company move at 4.30 p.m. and bivouacked at SANDPITS (E24 b 7.3) for the night. Orders were received in the morning to put the baths at MEAULTE to be put into working order. 2nd Lieuts McGILL and SINCLAIR were sent to see what required to be done, and afterwards took a party down to work.	JG
21/6/16		The Company was ready to move at 7.30 a.m., but it did not move until 9.60 a.m. The Company marched to MEAULTE and on the way were, with other troops on the march, bombed by German aeroplanes, but nothing resulted. One section started work on the bath houses at 6 a.m. and work was carried on during the day by reliefs.	JG
22/8/16		Orders were received that the mounted section, transport, and cyclists were to be ready to move off with 8th Brigade Transport at 10.40 a.m. Transport billeted for the night at POULAINVILLE. Dismounted section paraded for arms and equipment inspection. Work was continued on the baths.	JG
23/8/16		Orders were received at 12.30 a.m. for the dismounted section to entrain at MERICOURT at 6 a.m. The mounted section paraded at 3.45 a.m. and marched from MEAULTE to MERICOURT, and entrained. The mounted section arrived at FERNVILLERS-CARDAS at 11 a.m. and detrained and marched to EPECAMPS arriving there at 2.45 p.m. Mounted section and transport marched by road from POULAINVILLE to EPECAMPS arriving at 5.30 p.m.	JG
24/8/16		The Company remained in billets at EPECAMPS. Paraded in the morning for section drill. In the afternoon the company paraded for foot inspection. Orders were received to be ready to move on morning of 26th at 7.45 a.m.	JG

WAR DIARY
or
INTELLIGENCE SUMMARY

(Erase heading not required.)

Place	Date	Hour	Summary of Events and Information	Remarks and references to Appendices
			Sheet No 7.	
	25/8/16		CHESHIRE FIELD COY. R.E. Received notification that Capt. Holden granted inadequate leave on sick report (No AG 40). Coy. left EPECAMPS at 7.45 a.m. and joined 8th Brigade at BERNAVILLE Arrived at WAYANS at 11.45 a.m. and billeted there for night of 25/26. Foot inspection at 3 p.m. (Above in accordance with 8th Brig. Op. Or. No 6.) Rec. 8th Brig. Op. Or. No 62 to move on 26/8/16 at 3.30 p.m.	P.G.R.
	26/8/16		Coy. left WAYANS at 8.30 a.m. and joined 8th Brigade at BOFFLES Arrived at BLANGERMONT at 12 noon. Major J. WAYNE-MORGAN went sick at WAYANS at 8.0 a.m. and handed over command of Coy. to 2/Lt L.G. ROBERTSHAW. Coy. Billeted at BLANGERMONT for night of 26/27.	R.R.
	27/8/16		Coy. left BLANGERMONT at 7.45 a.m., joined 8th Brigade at RAMECOURT and arrived at TANGRY 3.30 p.m. delayed at railway grade crossings at RAMECOURT and ST POL. Billeted at TANGRY night 27/28.	P.G.R.
	28/8/16		Left TANGRY at 8.15 a.m. Joined 8th Brigade at Xroads south of PERNES arrived at BRUAY Cité No 7 at 2 p.m. Billeted at BRUAY night 28/29	P.G.R.

WAR DIARY or INTELLIGENCE SUMMARY

(Erase heading not required.)

SHEET No 8

Place	Date	Hour	Summary of Events and Information	Remarks and references to Appendices
	29/8/16		Orders received at 8.20 a.m. CHESHIRE FIELD COY. R.E. (No 65 (Br. op.o.) to relieve 152nd Fld Coy. R.E. at PHILOSOPHE. E. Coy left BRUAY at 11 a.m. and arrived PHILOSOPHE at 3 p.m. and took over work and billets occupied by 152nd Co. Dismounted portion of PHILOSOPHE. Mounted section and horse lines at MAZINGARBE.	J.W.G.
	30/8/16		Took over R.E. dump at FOSSE 3 and placed N.C.O. in charge. Reconnoitred Brigade area, Le Rutoire Alley (c.t.) to Barn Alley (c.t.) conducted by Captain STERN 15th Fld. Co. R.E. Made arrangements for use of trench railway FOSSE 3 to Quarry Dump with 283rd A.T. Co. R.E.	J.W.G.
	31/8/16		Reconnoitred bridge where track from LE RUTOIRE to making crosses LE RUTOIRE trench, with view to making in LONE TRENCH for forward billets. Reconnoitred dug-outs in allotment of work. Chas Fld Co R.E. to find out 8th Brig. requirements. Stationed permanent stat. keepers at Quarry R.E. Dump and Hay R.E. Dump R.E. dump at Fosse 3 taken over by R.S.M. PALMER.	J.W.G.

J.G. Whitehurst
Lt.R.
O.C. Cheshire for C.O. R.E.

3rd Divisional Engineers.

1/1ST CHESHIRE FIELD COMPANY R.E.

SEPTEMBER 1 9 1 6.

VOL 20.
Army Form C. 2118.

WAR DIARY
or
INTELLIGENCE SUMMARY

SEPTEMBER

Sheet Cheshire Fd Coy R.E.

Place	Date	Hour	Summary of Events and Information	Remarks and references to Appendices
			CHESHIRE FIELD COY. R.E.	VOL 20
	1/9/16		Started work on dug outs for forward billets in LONE TRENCH - 1 officer 1 section. Started work on S.T.G Emp in trench 68 at (H.19 a.2-1½) - 1 officer 1 section on reliefs of 6 hours. 2 sections worked on Foss 3 loading material to be taken by Lucks at night to Heap & Quarry Dumps, and repaired trucks. 4 sappers accompanied trucks, 1 officer in charge of train.	J.H.G.
	2/9/16		1 section on Lone Trench dugouts under Lt J Braddock, 1 section in 4+6h reliefs on S.G Emp at (H.19 a.2-15) under 2 Lt J Cottle. 2 Lts Thompson and Sinclair reconnoitred for M.T.M Emps at Cr. 7 and 72. 1 section returned in 4-6h reliefs on M.T.M Emplacement off O.T. 71 at (H.19 a.1-9). 1 section on odd jobs and clearing and fixing up billets and laying track in Foss 3. 4 sappers on material train to dumps. 3 horse wagons, 2 G.S. Limbers under Lt J Gourley went with material to GURREY DUMP.	J.H.G.
	3/9/16		1 section on Lone Trench dugouts. 1 section in 4-6h reliefs on S.G. Emp. 2 sections on M.T.M Emp at Jardin Ave. 1 section started on Stokes Gun Emplacement at Bargin 71 Lieut Woo attached officer & his work and both 50 men of 20 K.R.R and remaining section started at 10pm. 3 M.T.M Emps and 1 M.T.M Emp. working in 4-6 h. reliefs. Sites selected by Major Lieut Ommodie. M.T.M Battery and 2Lt W. Sinclair went away on 8 days special leave. Material to dumps by Ramway and Clos. Ford to R.E. Company.	J.H.G.

Army Form C. 2118.

WAR DIARY
or
INTELLIGENCE SUMMARY
(Erase heading not required.)

SHEET N° II

Place	Date	Hour	Summary of Events and Information	Remarks and references to Appendices
			CHESHIRE FIELD COY. R.E.	
	4/9/16		1 Section on Front Trench dugouts. 1 section on Stokes Gun Emp. 2 sections and 50 men 10th KRRs on 3 M.T.Ms and 1 H.T.M. Emp.s. Officers working on reliefs printed & comparison of all work in hand. Material taken to Posen and Hay R.E. dumps by mule transport and Ches. Fld Co. transport.	JhS.g.
	5/9/16		1 Section on Front Trench dugouts. 1 section on Stokes Gun Emp. FINISHED 2 sections and 50 men KRRs on 3 MTME and 1 HTME. 1 Section started on New HTME on HAY ALLEY. Material to dumps Hay and Posen by Tramway and Ches. Fld Co. transport.	JhS.g.
	6/9/16		1 Section on Front Trench dugouts, 2 sections and 50 KRRs on 3 MTMEs and 1 HTME. 1 Section on HTME on Hay Alley. Material to Hay and Posen Dumps by tramway and Ches. Fld Co. transport. Draft of 29 O.R.	JhS.g.
	7/9/16		arrived at 5pm from ROUEN via BETHUNE. 1 section on Front trench dugouts. 8 sappers and 200 infantry worked on HTM Emplacement. HAY ALLEY. 2 sections and 50 men KRRC on 3 MTM Emplacements. All worked in 4-6 hr reliefs. 32 sappers and 200 infantry started on Gun emplacements in front line from Boyau. 66 to 77A. 1 casualty - 1 O.R. wounded	JhS.g.
	8/9/16		8 sappers and 20 infantry on HTM Emp. 2 sections and 50 KRR on MTM Emps. 32 sappers and 200 infantry on preparing for Gun emplacements. 2	JhS.g.
	9/9/16		Two sections with 50 men KRRC on MTMEs 8 sappers and 20 infantry working on TM Emp HAY ALLEY in reliefs. 32 sappers and 200 infantry on Gun Emplacement in two shifts.	JhS.g.

Army Form C. 2118.

WAR DIARY or INTELLIGENCE SUMMARY
(Erase heading not required.)

SHEET III

Place	Date	Hour	Summary of Events and Information	Remarks and references to Appendices
			CHESHIRE FIELD COY. R.E	
	10/9/16		Two sections with 50 I.C.R.R in 4 - 6 ft. reliefs on 3 M.T.Ms and 2 H.T.M Emplacements. 24 sappers and 200 infantry on Gun emplacements by day. 32 sappers and 200 infantry on Gun emplacements by night.	J.h.G.
	11/9/16		Two sections and 50 K.R.R. in 4 - 6 ft. reliefs on 3 M.T.MEs on Essex Lane, Vendin Alley. Holly Lane completed. H.T.M on Vendin Alley completed. 24 sappers, 200 infantry working on emplas. Gun emplacements by day. 32 sappers 200 infantry working on Gun emplacements by night.	J.h.G.
	12/9/16		Work on H.T.M. Hay Alley stopped by Lt Snape, 3rd Div Trench Mortar Group Commander. Mining Co. R.E. completed third H.T.M Emp. was too near their sap head. 16 NCOs and sappers 150 infantry, 24 sappers and 100 infantry.	J.h.G.
	13/9/16		36 K.R.R. or Gun emplacements. 8 sappers and 30 infantry re commenced work on H.T.M Emp at Hay Alley. 3 sections R.E. 100 infantry and 48 I.C.R.R.s on Gun emplacements. Major F.L.N.Giles D.S.O. R.E. arrived Ex Rouen to 16.16 one command of Coy.	J.h.G.
	14/9/16		Sappers and 20 infantry on H.T.M. Emplacement Hay Alley. 1 NCO and 6 sappers on alterations to Philosophe Cemetery. 1 NCO and 4 sappers ret. tap. emplacement 6" in Front Line. Remainder of Coy. on improvement of billets.	Ages
	15/9/16		1 Sapper working with R.A.M.C. on August on St Georges Hospital. M.T.M. Emplacement in Hay Alley completed. 1 NCO and 6 sappers on alterations to Philosophe Cemetery. Work continued on M.T.M Emplacement off Holly Lane. Remainder of company erecting cookhouses, dining rooms workshops + generals improvement billets.	Ages

2449 Wt. W14957/M90 750,000 1/16 J.B.C. & A. Forms/C.2118/12.

WAR DIARY or INTELLIGENCE SUMMARY

Army Form C. 2118.

SHEET N° IV

CHESHIRE FIELD COY. R.E.

Place	Date	Hour	Summary of Events and Information	Remarks and references to Appendices
	16/9/16		1. Sappers erecting R.A.M.C. at advanced dressing station dug-out ST. GEORGE'S HOSPITAL. 2. Sappers and 5th K.R.R. pioneers working in continuous relief on M.T.M. Emplacement at HOLLY LANE. 1. N.C.O. and 6 Sappers on alterations to PHILOSOPHE Cemetery. 7. N.C.Os and 54 Sappers on additional rat-trap emplacements in FRONT LINE. Remainder of Coy. on improvements to billets. CAPTAIN P.Q. HENRIQUES joined the Coy. from ENGLAND. II LT. F.T. SINCLAIR rejoined the Coy. after leave.	Apps.
	17/9/16		Work continued on advanced dressing station on Aug. 1, M.T.M. Emplacement HOLLY LANE and alterations to PHILOSOPHE Cemetery. Extra rat-traps in FRONT LINE. Work commenced on deep dug-out for Lewis gunners in FRONT LINE near BOYAU 75 and Brigade Headquarters Battle Dug-out in LONE TRENCH. Improvements to billets continued.	Apps.
	18/9/16		Work continued in M.T.M. Emplacement HOLLY LANE + deep dug-out for Lewis Gunners in FRONT LINE. All available pioneers employed in afternoon on just completed rat-trap emplacements in FRONT LINE.	Apps.
	19/9/16		Work continued on M.T.M. Emplacement HOLLY LANE and deep dug-out for Lewis Gunners in FRONT LINE. New Brigade Headquarters Battle dug-out in LONE TRENCH Improvements to billets continued. 4 Sappers joined from BASE.	Apps.
	20/9/16		Work commenced as for 19/9/16 - cancelled at noon. All Sappers and N.C.O. and K.R.R. party attached for work were employed at night wiring in front of FRONT LINE. Orders received to hand over to the 2nd Field Coy R.E. at 10am - 21/9/16.	Apps.
	21/9/16		Attack of work in hand, maps etc. & information as to working arrangements handed over to 2nd Field Co. R.E. at 1 pm. The Company employed in looking longers in afternoon. Orders received to meet the 9th Brigade at MOUEX-LES-MINES at 8.15 am on 22/9/16.	Apps.
	22/9/16		Left PHILOSOPHE at 6.45 a.m. & joined the 9th Brigade at MOUEX-LES-MINES at 8.15 am. The Coy proceeded to AUCHEL arriving at 1.15 pm where it was billeted. Orders to move received at 11.45 pm.	Apps.
	23/9/16		The Coy. left AUCHEL at 8.10 am en route to AUDINGTHUM. Orders received en route to proceed to & billet in MATRINGHEM. The Company arrived in MATRINGHEM at 4 pm. & was billeted there.	Apps.

Army Form C. 2118.

WAR DIARY
or
INTELLIGENCE SUMMARY
(Erase heading not required.)

Instructions regarding War Diaries and Intelligence Summaries are contained in F.S. Regs., Part II. and the Staff Manual respectively. Title Pages will be prepared in manuscript.

SHEET No V.

CHESHIRE FIELD COY. R.E.

Place	Date	Hour	Summary of Events and Information	Remarks and references to Appendices
	24/9/16		The Company paraded & drilled in the morning. Clean arms & gas helmets inspection at 2 pm. The Officers were engaged in selecting sites for company training.	J.A.S.
	25/9/16		Infantry training and musketry instruction in the morning. Musketry practice carried out by the entire Company in the afternoon.	J.A.S.
	26/9/16		Clean arms inspection. Lecture by Capt P.Q. HENRIQUES on "Siting of Trenches" & "Siting of Work". 2 Officers of the R.S.F. attended for instruction. The Coy. was practised in "Siting of Trenches" & "Laying out of Work" by Section Officers in the afternoon. 2/LT L.G. ROBERTSHAW left for ENGLAND via BOULOGNE on leave.	J.A.S.
	27/9/16		Clean arms inspection. Lecture on "Strong Points and Redoubts". The Company was practised in construction of Strong Points, Redoubts & the Laying of Wire Entanglements. Junior Officers of Infantry Officers in Siting of Strong Points, Redoubts & the Laying of Wire Entanglements. Junior Officers of Infantry, Capt. in the Brigade attended for instruction. Bathing Parade in the afternoon. Infantry & R.E. for Junior N.C.Os.	J.A.S.
	28/9/16		Clean arms inspection. Lecture on "The Construction of Obstacles". The Company visited the field works constructed in RADINGHEM for instruction; & was practised in the use of planks & line. Infantry Officers attended as on previous days. Bridging material & toploures overhauled in the afternoon.	J.A.S.
	29/9/16		Lecture on "The Defence of Works & Villages". The Company was engaged in schemes for the defence of the Woods & Villages in the vicinity under the Section Officers; & also on the preparation & reconnaissance of reports.	J.A.S.
	30/9/16		Lecture on "Bridging Equipment". The Company was practised in Pontoon Bridging "take the line" & Welhan Trestle on the quarry pits in MATRINGHEM.	J.A.S.

Army Form C. 2118.

WAR DIARY
or
INTELLIGENCE SUMMARY

SEPTEMBER 1916   SHEET No VII

(Erase heading not required.)

Place	Date	Hour	Summary of Events and Information	Remarks and references to Appendices
			Awards - The following N.C.O's CHESHIRE FIELD COY. R.E. have been awarded the Military Medal. viz:— No 146 Acting Sergt. EASON, R. No 350 Acting Lce/Cpl. JONES, R. No 990 Acting Lce/Cpl. SAGE, G.P., during the present month.	Appx. J.Miles C Major R.E. Comdg Ches...

3rd Divisional Engineers.

1/1ST CHESHIRE FIELD COMPANY R.E.

OCTOBER 1916.

Army Form C. 2118.

"1/1 Cheshire F. Coy"

WAR DIARY
or
INTELLIGENCE SUMMARY

OCTOBER 1916

SHEET No. 1   Vol 21

Instructions regarding War Diaries and Intelligence Summaries are contained in F.S. Regs., Part II. and the Staff Manual respectively. Title Pages will be prepared in manuscript.

Place	Date	Hour	Summary of Events and Information	Remarks and references to Appendices
			"CHESHIRE FIELD COY. R.E."	
	1/10/16		The Company rested in MATRINGHEM. Church Parade for all denominations.	J.C.S.
	2/10/16		Lecture on "Pontooning" & "Weldon Trestle Bridging" followed by practice on RIVER LYS.	J.C.S.
	3/10/16		Lecture on "Demolitions". The Company was afterwards exercised in the use of explosives.	J.C.S.
	4/10/16		The Company took part in Divisional Exercises in COYECQUE. Orders received at 11.45 p.m. to leave MATRINGHEM.	J.C.S.
	5/10/16		The Company left MATRINGHEM at 12 noon & proceeded to & were billeted in PREDEFIN. Company at 3.30 p.m.	J.C.S.
	6/10/16		The Mounted Section & Transport left PREDEFIN at 8.30 a.m. & arrived at PETIT BOURET at 6.30 p.m. when it was billeted for the night. The Remainder of the Company stayed in PREDEFIN.	J.C.S.
	7/10/16		Train of left PETIT BOURET at 6.45 a.m. for HALVILLERS, where it arrived at 5.30 p.m. The Remainder of the Company left PREDEFIN at 1 p.m. for ACHEUX where it arrived at 9 p.m.	J.C.S.
	8/10/16		Orders received at 7.30 a.m. to transport to proceed to MAILLY-MAILLET via ACHEUX. The Company was billeted in MAILLY-MAILLET from midnight 8-9/10/16.	J.C.S.
	9/10/16		Work taken over from EAST ANGLIAN FD. CO. R.E. in the SERRE SECTOR.	J.C.S.
	10/10/16		The Company was engaged in making dugouts ROB ROY TRENCH, Brigade Battle Headquarters in DUNNOW TRENCH & RAILWAY AVENUE, also improving O.T. & fixing sign boards & work in connection with the Water Supply. 2 Lt. L.G. ROBERTSHAW returned from leave.	J.C.S.
	11/10/16		Port to her 10/10/16 was continued. The Command of the Company was handed over to CAPTAIN F.Q. HENRIQUES R.E.(T)	J.C.S.

WAR DIARY
or
INTELLIGENCE SUMMARY

(Erase heading not required.)

Army Form C. 2118.

SHEET No. 2

Place	Date	Hour	Summary of Events and Information	Remarks and references to Appendices
			CHESHIRE FIELD COY. R.E.	
	14/10/16		The Company was engaged in continuous relays on dug-outs in DUNMOW and ROB ROY TRENCHES, improving the trenches in the SOUTHERN SECTOR, making wire boards, loading transport & on water supply duties	1/1/1/S
	15/10/16		Work as per 14/10/16 was continued. Major F.L.N. GILES, D.S.O., R.E., left the Company to take up duties with the 2nd Army.	1/1/1/S
	14/10/16		Work continued in the construction of dug-outs, repair of trenches, formation of ½ Battalion dumps & water supply duties	1/1/1/S
	15/10/16		Work continued. A Church Parade for available men of all denominations was held, for R.C's at 11 a.m. & for C. of E. at 4 p.m.	1/1/1/S
	16/10/16		Work as per 14/10/16 was continued. The Company carried work on the ROB ROY dug-outs at 1 p.m. O.S.M. QUIGLAT received White Card in Recognition of services rendered.	1/1/1/S
	17/10/16		The Company was engaged on Brigade Battle H.Q. DUNMOW TRENCH, repairing trenches in the SOUTHERN SECTOR and on Water Supply duties. Received movement orders at midnight.	1/1/1/S
	18/10/16		Work continued on Brigade Battle H.Q. DUNMOW TRENCH. The Company left MAILLY-MAILLET at 11 a.m. & proceeded to COURCELLES-AU-BOIS where it was lodged in tents & bivouacs.	1/1/1/S
	19/10/16		Work continued on Brigade Battle H.Q., repairing trenches in SOUTHERN SECTOR & Water Supply duties. Horse lines removed from BEAUSART to COURCELLES-AU-BOIS	1/1/1/S
	20/10/16		Work continued on Brigade Battle H.Q., repairing trenches in SOUTHERN SECTOR, carrying materials for "S" dump & Water Supply duties. The Military Medal Ribbon was presented to SERGT. A. JONES. 3 reinforcement E. O.R. joined the Company.	1/1/1/S
	21/10/16		Work continued on Brigade Battle H.Q., repairing trenches in the SOUTHERN SECTOR, carrying materials for "S" dump, making pack saddlery & on Water Supply duties. 1 O.R. wounded.	1/1/1/S
	22/10/16		Work continued as per 21/10/16.	1/1/1/S

Army Form C. 2118.

WAR DIARY
or
INTELLIGENCE SUMMARY

(Erase heading not required.)

SHEET No. 3.

Place	Date	Hour	Summary of Events and Information	Remarks and references to Appendices
			CHESHIRE FIELD COY. R.E.	
	23/10/16		The Company was engaged on Brigade Battle H.Q. OUNMOW TRENCH, repairing trenches in SOUTHERN AVENUE, or Heavy T.M. dugout in GREY ST, carrying materials for T.M. Emplacements in ROB ROY, & on water supply duties & the making of pack saddlery. II. LT. F.T. SINCLAIR left & took up duties with the Royal Flying Corps.	A/J.W.S.
	24/10/16		Work was continued on Brigade Battle H.Q., repairing trenches in SOUTHERN SECTOR, carrying materials to Stokes gun emplacement in FRONT LINE, on water supply duties & the making of pack saddlery.	A/J.W.S.
	25/10/16		Work was continued on Brigade Battle H.Q., repairing trenches in SOUTHERN SECTOR, water supply duties & the making of pack saddlery.	A/J.W.S.
	26/10/16		Brigade Battle H.Q. completed. Work continued on repairs to trenches in SOUTHERN SECTOR, carrying materials to "S" dump, making pack saddlery & water supply duties.	A/J.W.S.
	27/10/16		The Company was engaged on repairs to trenches in the SOUTHERN SECTOR, carrying materials to "S" dump & on water supply duties. 1. O.R. killed.	J.W.S.
	28/10/16		Work continued on trench maintenance and repairs in the SOUTHERN SECTOR, carrying material to "S" dump & water supply duties.	J.W.S.
	29/10/16		Work continued as per 28/10/16.	J.W.S.
	30/10/16		Work continued as per 29/10/16. Reinforcements 2 O.R. from the BASE.	J.W.S.
	31/10/16		Work continued as per 30/10/16. II. LT. F. COTTLE left the Company & took up duties with the Army Service Corps.	J.W.S.

P.Q. Henriques Capt.
Comdg. Ches. Fld. Coy. R.E.

1-11-16

War Diary.

SECRET Copy No 6 № 27
23 x 1916

1/1 Cheshire Field Coy Orders

1. During the forthcoming operations the 1/1 Cheshire Field Co RE (less 1 officer + 10 OR detailed for Water Supply Duties) will be allotted to 8th Inf Brigade to assist in putting the village of SERRE into a state of defence.

The Field Co RE assisted by B Coy of 20th KRRC (Pioneers) will carry out the following work:-

(a) Prepare at each of the points ABCDEF (shown on sheet attached) about 40 yards of Fire trench with emplacements of 2 M Guns. 4 MG (Vickers) will be placed in these strong points in situations to be selected by the Commandant Capt N.Y. TYLE 1st R I Fus

(b) Wire a single line of French wire with screw pickets and barbed wire as shown on sketch about 200 yards in length & about 30 yards distant from each of the above strong points

(c) Straighten communication trenches leading into SERRE for about 40 yards outside the above strong points to prevent bombing attacks. On completion of the above, continue

Copy No 6   M.27
23 V 1916

consolidation of perimeter of JERRE joining up the above strong points with fire trench and wire and then continue along South East face.

The Garrison consisting of 2 Companies of the R.S. Fus. will assist in this work.

(d) Clear communication trenches inside the village and if a suitable locality can be found a Keep will be constructed.

(e) Five wells are said to exist and 2 buckets and 2 1" ropes 200' long will be carried by the Field Coy & the company of Pioneers.

The parties have been allotted to Strong Points as follows:-

A   1 Platoon   20th KRRC Pioneers
B   1 Platoon   "   "
C   2 Sections   Khestine Field Coy R E
D   2 Sections   "   "
E   1 Platoon   20th KRRC Pioneers
F   1 Platoon   "   "

A seventh strong point may be required on the South East face of the village about 130 yards West of the Strong Point A. Instructions regarding this will be issued later.

2. An infantry carrying party of 50 men under the command of Lt. D.G. INNES.

Copy No 6 DT 27
23 X 1916

8th East Yorks Regt will carry material from the forward RE Dumps to a point selected in the village of SERRE. 2nd Lt MILNES will go forward with the first working party.

The assembly position of the 1/1 Cheshire Field Coy RE, B Coy 20th KRRC (Pioneers) and the carrying party 50 men will be HITTITE Trench & GRISIGNY Farm ✕

The whole party will go forward on receipt of orders from 8th Inf Brigade

2nd Lt J. MCG 1th (and 2 runners) is detailed to report to 8th Inf Brigade Battle HQrs at 9 pm on Y day. This officer to remain with 8th Inf Brigade throughout the operations or until permitted to return to No 1 Section

5. The position of the two ½ Battalion Dumps is K29 c 2 9 on SOUTHERN Trench between MONK and ROB ROY. RE Material Dumps are by the ½ Battalion Dumps

6. The position of the CRE will be at the Divisional Advanced Head Qrs Dugouts in SOUTHERN Avenue

The position of the 8th Brigade HQrs is K28 C 45.00 in DUNMOW Trench near RAILWAY AVENUE.

✕ With Dugouts Hegean between REY Alleys & NORTHERN ....

Copy No. 6   M27
23 x 1916

7 There will be Regimental Aid Posts at :-
    SPRING   K 29 c 05 75
    SUMMER   K 28 d 8 9
    AUTUMN + WINTER   K 28 b 75.30

8 References made in orders to maps will refer to Map 1/20000 Sheet K17-M21 and 1/10,000 and 1/5000 Trench Maps. The 1/20,000 Trench Map Edition 1 will be the map used in all messages from Units to 8th Inf Brigade and from Brigade to Units as regards Enemy Lines

Note :- No documents or letters, official or private are to be carried on the person when going into action. The only maps allowed are the ones shewing the German Trenches but containing nothing alluding to our Trenches or to our objective or maps shewing the country in which operations are taking place.

9 All ranks will have the Divisional Mark sewn on the haversack and wear the white shoulder tape used by the R E in operations :-

10 Each man will wear fighting order :-
    (a) Full Water Bottle. This is most important
    (b) 2 days Rations
    (c) 50 Rounds of Ammunition
    (d) 15 Sandbags
    (e) Waterproof Sheet
        Great Coat in Bandoole

Copy No 6   M27
23 × 1916

1. Each party for work on the six strong points will be organized as follows:-
Points AB = E F 1 platoon Pioneers 8 Inf carryg party.
   "   CD   2 Section RE   8   "   "   "

2. Each party will carry forward the following stores.
   30 Shovels   24 Small Pickets
   10 Picks   300 Yards Tracing Tape
   2 Axes
   1 Bar
   6 Wirecutters
   12 Pairs Gloves
   2 Buckets   } per Field Coy R.E.
   2 200' 1" Ropes } + Coy K.R.R.C.

3. The carrying party will bring per party of 8 men:-
        4 Coils French Wire (15 yards each)
        2 "   Barbed Wire
        6 Screw Pickets.

When these materials are delivered to the site of each strong point the parties of 8 men will be reorganized as 1 combined carrying party under 2 Lt MILNES to bring materials of the above wire entanglement requirements from the RE Dump at K 29 c 2 9 on SOUTHERN Avenue between MONK & ROB ROY Trench

Copy No 6   M27
23. X. 1916

and deposit stores to form an R E D ump
in the village of SERRE

14. The working parties will remain at work
until the consolidation is completed.

15. The attention of all is drawn to the following:—
(a) All men must be made to exercise
restraint in the matter of drinking from
their water bottles. It is quite probable that
the only water obtainable during the 24 hours
will be that carried in the water bottles.
No water should be touched in the German
lines until it has been examined by a
Medical Officer and declared free from
poison

(b) The word "Retire" does not exist and
will not be understood or obeyed by
anyone in the Brigade. When once the
advance has begun all ranks must be
imbued with the spirit of going on
their objective

c No unwounded man is to be allowed on
any account to bring back wounded men
during the attack. Wounded able to walk
will make their way to the Regimental Aid
Post. Men unable to walk must await
the stretcher bearers who cannot come up
until the advancing lines have passed on

Copy No. 6   JR 27
23 x 1916

Unwounded men found bringing back wounded during the attack will be treated as stragglers.

16. II Lt H.J.F GOURLEY will be in charge of the Company Transport.
He will arrange for 2 Pontoon Waggons & 1 Trestle Wagon to stand by ready to bring up any material required on Z day from ~~JEROLtm~~ ERO hm onwards.
He will await instructions in the road outside Cheshire Field by R.E. Bivouacs COURCELLES.

17. II Lt F COTTLE will remain with Company Head Qrs and take charge of all papers, money, etc.

18. II Lt H.A BRADDOCK will be employed with 10 sappers upon Water Supply Duties in accordance with preliminary instructions issued on the 17th inst. in JR 16.

19. Sections 2 & 4 under the command of II Lt ROBERTSHAW will work on strong point C.
Sections 1 & 3 under the command of II Lt THOMPSON will work upon strong point D.

20. The Sections must turn out to their maximum strength.

Copy No 6   IM 27
23.x.1916.

A headquarters guard being provided by details of Cooks, Batmen & Tool Cart men - in charge of the C.S.M.

21   In the event of the OC 1/1 Cheshire Field Coy R E becoming a casualty the next senior RE officer will take charge of the defensive works & issue instructions to ~~co-operation with~~ the OC "B" Coy 20th K R R C Pioneers

22   Please acknowledge

P.Q. Henriques
Capt. RE (T)
Comdg Cheshire Field Co RE

Papers attached
(a) Map of SERRE showing strong points
    A B C D E F   1/2500
(b) Information regarding houses in SERRE

Copies Nos. 1 + 3 to CRE 3rd Division
            4 + 5   8th Inf Brigade
            6   War Diary
            7 + 8   OC B Coy K R R C
            9, 10, 11   Cheshire Field Co RE
            2   File

Copy No. 6.

SECRET

Amendment to 4th Cheshire Field Coy RE Orders of 23.x.1916.

Para 19. For "Sections 2+4" read "Sections 1+2"
For "Sections 1+3" read "Sections 3+4"

P.O. Hawkes
Capt. RE(T)
26/10/16   Comdg Cheshire Field Coy R.E.

                                                                52
                                                          M.28.

Receipt of Operation Orders.

Nº 1 & 3.   C.R.E. ack⁰. 84C
                                    23.x.16.

4 & 5.   8th Inf Bde.   23 x 16 PGH

2.   file.   PGH 24/10/16

6.   War Diary.   PGH 24/10/16

9   2Lt. McGill.   J McGill 24/10/16

10.   2Lt. Thompson.   SGT 24/10/16

11.   2Lt. Braddock.   HyaS 24/10/16

A.   2Lt. Milnes. E.E. Yorks. TWM 24/10/16

B.   2Lt. F. Cottle.   FC. 24/10/16

C.   2Lt. Gousley.   HJS 24/10/16

7 & 8.   O.C. B Coy KRRC   signed 24/10/16
                                     HARAWA

D.   2Lt. Robertshaw   OC. B Coy 24/10/16

24 x 1916.

SECRET   Copy No 6.   No 4

Amendment to 1/1 Cheshire Field Co RE
Orders of 23.X.1916

Para 12: Add "any men of the parties
not carrying tools will carry
materials for French bar wire
entanglement."

P.O. Hewoquies Capt RE (?)
25.X.16.   Comdg 1st Cheshire Field Co RE

3rd Divisional Engineers.

1/1ST CHESHIRE FIELD COMPANY R.E.

NOVEMBER 1 9 1 6.

WAR DIARY
or
INTELLIGENCE SUMMARY

Army Form C. 2118.

NOVEMBER 1916   SHEET N°1.

Place	Date	Hour	Summary of Events and Information	Remarks and references to Appendices
			CHESHIRE FIELD COY. R.E.	
	1/11/16		The Company was engaged in clearing & draining RAILWAY AV. SOUTHERN AV. & HITTITE TR. by day & SOUTHERN AV. by night, & on water supply duties & room repairs. MONK.	J.G.S.
	2/11/16		Work continued in clearing RAILWAY AV. SOUTHERN AV. & TAUPIN by day, SOUTHERN AV. GUNNER TR & BLENEAU by night, the erection of a drying shed in COURCELLES, & water supply duties.	J.G.S.
	3/11/16		Work continued on trench draining & maintenance as per 2/11/16, also in making trench boards & U frames; the erection of a drying shed & hut & in water supply duties.	J.G.S.
	4/11/16		The Company left the bivouacs & moved into billets in COURCELLES. Work continued on clearing trenches as per 3/11/16, water supply duties & making a hut for 8th Inf. Bgde.	J.G.S.
	5/11/16		Work continued on trench maintenance in SOUTHERN SECTOR, making trench boards & huts & on water supply duties.	J.G.S.
	6/11/16		The Company was engaged in improving C.T.'s in SOUTHERN SECTOR, making latrines & baths steps, huts for 8th Bgde. water supply duties & hutting in VAUCHELLES.	J.G.S.

WAR DIARY
or
INTELLIGENCE SUMMARY

(Erase heading not required.)

Army Form C. 2118.

SHEET Nº 2.

CHESHIRE FIELD COY, R.E.

Place	Date	Hour	Summary of Events and Information	Remarks and references to Appendices
	7/10/16		The Company was engaged in repairing C.T's in the SOUTHERN SECTOR, repairing dug-outs & Bgde. H.Q. in DUNMOW & MONK, making hut for 8th Bgde; hutting in VAUCHELLES & on water supply duties.	J.g.a.S.
	8/10/16		Work continued in improving repairing C.T.S, preparing fire bays in MONK TR: making hut for 8th Bgde; hutting in VAUCHELLES & on water supply duties.	J.g.a.S.
	9/10/16		Work continued on repairs to trenches west of SACKVILLE ST: water supply duties & hutting in VAUCHELLES	J.g.a.S.
	10/10/16		Took entered cookers 9/10/16 & in making fire bays in MONK TR. & trench boards	J.g.a.S.
	11/10/16		The Company was engaged in clearing & draining MONK TR & ROB ROY, improving C.T's in the SOUTHERN SECTOR, clearing & repairing dug-outs in DUNMOW, making hut for 8th Bgde & on water Supply duties.	J.g.a.S.
	12/10/16		Rode from Authuille to LA SIGNY FARM. The Coy. proceeded to assembly from	(sd)
	13/10/16		After exploration the Coy remained all day at LA SIGNY & returned to Billets in evening having done nothing	O.P.

WAR DIARY
or
INTELLIGENCE SUMMARY

Army Form C. 2118.

SHEET No 3.

Place	Date	Hour	Summary of Events and Information	Remarks and references to Appendices
	14/4/16 15/4/16		CHESHIRE FIELD COY. R.E. 2 sections wiring front + front line. Remainder making U frames etc.	(AB)
	14/4/16		Work on C.T.'s repaired.	(AB)
	16/4/16 18/4/16		Work in C.T.'s. Commenced making U frames for revetting.	(AB)
	19/4/16 20/4/16		Commenced work in MONK Tr. (S. of FLAG) clearing for U frames.	(AB)
	21/4/16		Above work continued. (Night work)	(AB)
	22/4/16 23/4/16		Site of above work changed from MONK Tr. to Ist (word) running just in front. Clearing commenced. Above work continued. V.A.C. commenced erection of NISSEN huts in COURCELLES, taken over from R.A.R.E.	(AB)
	24/4/16 to 30/4/16		Night work in front MONK Tr. continued. (Framing with U frames + revetting with C.G.I. exp. metal) 1 Sec. still working on NISSEN huts in COURCELLES.	(AB)

Casualties

| | 3/4/16 4/4/16 | | Capt. F.A. HENRIQUES (Wounded (Shell shock) 4/4/16. 6 O.R. Killed. 8 O.R. Wounded (2 since died) 2 O.R. Wounded. 2/Lt. A.B. CLOUGH R.E. joined | (AB) (AB) |
| | 13/4/16 17/4/16 | | 2/Lt. J.W. BLAIKIE joined. | (AB) |

R.B. Sly? Capt. R.E.
Cheshire
OC Cheshire 30/4/16

3rd Divisional Engineers.

1/1st CHESHIRE FIELD COMPANY R.E.

DECEMBER 1 9 1 6.

Army Form C. 2118.

WAR DIARY
or
INTELLIGENCE SUMMARY
(Erase heading not required.)

DECEMBER 1916   SHEET 1

Place	Date	Hour	Summary of Events and Information	Remarks and references to Appendices
			CHESHIRE FIELD COY. R.E.	
	1/12/16		The Company was engaged as follows: 2 Sections framing, roofing, retaining MONK TRENCH, 1 Section erecting NISSEN HUTS in COURCELLES, remainder working in R.E. Park, EUSTON DUMP & on water supply duties.	Appx.S
	2/12/16		Work continued in repair of MONK TRENCH, erection of huts in COURCELLES, making frames etc in R.E. Park and water supply duties.	Appx.S
	3/12/16		2 Sections repairing MONK TRENCH, 1 Sect. erecting huts, remainder of Coy. engaged in R.E. Park, in water supply duties & at EUSTON DUMP. LT. A.W. DAVIES and 2/LT G.A. MANNING joined the Coy. from the Base	Appx.S
			⊕ North continued as per 3/12/16. CAPTN J.P. WARD joined the Coy. from the Base	Appx.S
	4/12/16			
	5/12/16		The Company was engaged in erecting huts in COURCELLES, repairing MONK TRENCH, making frames etc in R.E. Park and on water supply duties.	Appx.S
	6/12/16		The Company was engaged in repairing MONK TRENCH, erecting huts in COURCELLES, repairing machine gunners dug-out in LEGEND TRENCH, making frames etc in R.E. Park. On water supply duties.	Appx.S
	7/12/16		The Company was engaged in repairing MONK TRENCH, erecting huts in COURCELLES, repairing dug-outs in LEGEND TRENCH and FLAG AVENUE, making french frames & on water supply duties.	Appx.S
	8/12/16		CAPTAIN J.P. WARD, R.E.(T) took over the Command of the Coy. from CAPTN. A.B. CLOUGH, R.E. who rejoined the 56th Company R.E. Work was continued as per 7/12/16	Appx.S

Army Form C. 2118.

WAR DIARY
or
INTELLIGENCE SUMMARY

(Erase heading not required.)

DECEMBER 1916   SHEET 2

Place	Date	Hour	Summary of Events and Information	Remarks and references to Appendices
			"CHESHIRE FIELD COY. R.E.	
	9/12/16		The Company has been engaged in repairing MONK TRENCH, erecting huts in COURCELLES, repairing dugouts in LEGEND TR: and FLAG AV: making trench frames and in water supply duties	Sgs.S.
	10/12/16		Work was continued as per 9/12/16	Sgs.S.
	11/12/16		Work was continued in repairing MONK TRENCH, erecting huts in COURCELLES, repairing dugouts in LEGEND TR: and FLAG AV: making trench frames + duck boards, in water supply duties	Sgs.S.
	12/12/16		The Company was engaged in repairing MONK TRENCH, erecting huts etc. in COURCELLES, repairing dug-outs in LEGEND TR + FLAG AV: making trench frames + duck boards in water supply duties	Sgs.S.
	13/12/16		Work was continued as per 12/12/16	Sgs.S.
	14/12/16		The Company was engaged in repairing MONK TRENCH, making trench frames etc, repairing dug-outs in LEGEND TR: and FLAG AV: erecting huts, repairing billets etc in COURCELLES, in water supply duties	Sgs.S.
	15/12/16		Work continued as per 14/12/16	Sgs.S.
	16/12/16		The Company was engaged in erecting huts etc in COURCELLES, repairing dug-outs in LEGEND TR: and FLAG AV: making trench frames + boards, repairing MONK TRENCH in water supply duties	Sgs.S.
	17/12/16		Work was continued in repairing MONK TR: making trench frames + boards, erecting huts etc in COURCELLES, repairing dug-outs in LEGEND TR: and FLAG AV: and in water supply duties	Sgs.S.

Army Form C. 2118.

WAR DIARY
or
INTELLIGENCE SUMMARY
(Erase heading not required.)

DECEMBER 1916   SHEET 3

Instructions regarding War Diaries and Intelligence Summaries are contained in F.S. Regs., Part II and the Staff Manual respectively. Title Pages will be prepared in manuscript.

Place	Date	Hour	Summary of Events and Information	Remarks and references to Appendices
CHESHIRE FIELD COY. R.E.				
	18/12/16		The Company was engaged in repairing dug-outs in LEGEND TR. and FLAG AV., erecting huts in COURCELLES, repairing MONK TR., making frames etc. in R.E. Park and in water supply duties	J.H.C.J.S.
	19/12/16		Work continued in repairs to dug-outs in LEGEND TR. and FLAG AV, hutting etc. in COURCELLES, repairing MONK TR., making frames etc. in R.E. Park and water supply duties.	J.H.C.J.S.
	20/12/16		The Company was engaged in repairing MONK TR. dugouts in LEGEND TR. and FLAG AV., erecting huts in COURCELLES, making frames etc. in R.E. Park and in water supply duties.	J.H.C.J.S.
	21/12/16		Work was continued as per 20/12/16	J.H.C.J.S.
	22/12/16		Work was continued in repairing MONK TR. and dugouts in LEGEND TR. and FLAG AV., erecting huts in COURCELLES, water supply duties and work in the R.E. Park	J.H.C.J.S.
	23/12/16		The Company was engaged in water supply duties, making frames etc. in R.E. Park, erecting huts in COURCELLES, repairing dug-outs in LEGEND TR. and FLAG AV. and repairing MONK and FLAG Trenches	J.H.C.J.S.
	24/12/16		Work was continued as per 23/12/16	J.H.C.J.S.
	25/12/16		By order of the Corps Commander work was suspended on this day, except for matters requiring very urgent attention	J.H.C.J.S.
	26/12/16		The Company was engaged in repairing MONK & FLAG Trenches, erecting huts in COURCELLES, repairing dug-outs in LEGEND TR. and FLAG AV., water supply duties & work in the R.E. Park	J.H.C.J.S.

Army Form C. 2118.

WAR DIARY or INTELLIGENCE SUMMARY

(Erase heading not required.)

DECEMBER SHEET. 4.

Place	Date	Hour	Summary of Events and Information	Remarks and references to Appendices
"CHESHIRE FIELD COY. R.E.	27/12/16		The Company was engaged in repairing MONK Trench and Avy Cnt. FLAG Tr. Repairing Avy Cuts in SACKVILLE and LEGEND Trenches erecting huts in COURCELLES making tramways in R.E. PARK and on trench supply duties.	MM
	28/12/16		Work was continued as on the 27/12/16 and hutting commenced in the DELL.	MM
	29/12/16		Work was continued in repairing MONK Tr. & approach in LEGEND Tr. SACKVILLE Av. & FLAG Av. Erecting huts in COURCELLES and the DELL making tramways in R.E. PARK and trench supply duties.	MM
	30/12/16		Work was continued as on the 28/12/16. Party also engaged in chipping out Dugout in MONK Tr. Blown in by shell fire.	MM
	31/12/16		Relief operations carried out on chipping out Dugouts in MONK Tr. hutting. Re form hutting in COURCELLES and the DELL making trams in R.E. PARK and making supply dutis. Repairing Dugouts in SACKVILLE Av and LEGEND Tr.	MM

Army Form C. 2118.

WAR DIARY
or
INTELLIGENCE SUMMARY
(Erase heading not required.)

DECEMBER SHEET 5

Place	Date	Hour	Summary of Events and Information	Remarks and references to Appendices
CHESHIRE FIELD COY. R.E				
			CASUALTIES	
			Wounded. I.O.R. 22/12/16	
			Awards	
			532 Actg Coyl Sergt Trenton J. } Awarded Meritous	MM
			534 2nd " Sergeant Wright R.O. } Service from General	
			508 " Sergeant Jones H. } Routine from General	MM
			363 " Sapper Turnbank E.R. } Good services	
			Officers Joining	
			Lieut ! Lt. A.W. Davies 3/12/16	MM
			2Lt. G.A. Fanning 3/12/16	
			Capt. L.R. Ward 4/12/16	
			Officers Leaving	
			Lieut ! Capt. A.B. Ebert 8/12/16 John Chamblyn MM	
			O.C. Cheshire Field Coy.	

3rd Division
War Diaries
438th Cheshire Field Coy
January To 31st December
1917

Army Form C. 2118.

WAR DIARY or INTELLIGENCE SUMMARY
(Erase heading not required.)

JANUARY 1917

Place	Date	Hour	Summary of Events and Information	Remarks and references to Appendices
			"CHESHIRE FIELD COY. R.E."	
	1/1/17		By order of Corps Commander work was suspended on this day except to give this urgent attention. Sixth party were engaged digging out MONK Trench blown in by shell fire.	JM.
	2/1/17		The Company were engaged as follows: 2 Sections ramming revetting and clearing MONK TRENCH. One section revetting NISSEN HUTS at THE DEPOT making frames in R.E. Park, making supports etc. One section repairing dug outs in LEGEND Tr. and SACKVILLE St.	JM.
	3/1/17		Work continued as per 2/1/17. 63 C.S.M. QUIGLEY awarded D.C.M.	JM.
	4/1/17		The Company were engaged in repairing MONK TRENCH and busy tools in THE DELL, making frames in R.E. Park, making supply and repairing Dug Outs FLAG AVENUE, LEGEND TRENCH and SACKVILLE STREET. No 56559 Sapr for LOGGINS.	JM.
	5/1/17		Work continued as per 4/1/17, also 14 men engaged assembling post No 28 Frame 35. C. captured this day from the Enemy	JM.
	6/1/17		The Company were engaged in trench Patrol duties repairing and clearing dug outs, elevating in top shell line at Ref. 80.5.B1.6.65. Section of 218th Field Coy R.E. took over work on Dug outs and Railway.	JM.

WAR DIARY or INTELLIGENCE SUMMARY

Army Form C. 2118.

JANUARY 1917 Sheet No 2

Place	Date	Hour	Summary of Events and Information	Remarks and references to Appendices
CHESHIRE FIELD COY. R.E.	7/1/17		The Company has two sections engaged in works, burial and repair of MONK TRENCH. The party engaged on MONK TRENCH had several hits and narrow escapes owing to heavy enemy shelling.	JM
	8/1/17		Company has two sections engaged on forming dugouts and other employment, duties and work on front line trenches handed over to the 210th Field Coy R.E.	JM
	9/1/17		The Company has been section left BOURCELLES en route for PUCHEVILLERS. Received PUCHEVILLERS at 6 P.M. and was billeted for the night there.	JM
	10/1/17		Company proceeded to LANCHES arrived at 6 P.M. and were billeted by 7 P.M.	JM
	11/1/17		Usual work held and little employment	JM
	12/1/17		Usual works, inspection held & company engaged on temporary defences	JM

Army Form C. 2118.

WAR DIARY
or
INTELLIGENCE SUMMARY
(Erase heading not required.)

JANUARY 1917 Feather 3

Place	Date	Hour	Summary of Events and Information	Remarks and references to Appendices
			CHESHIRE FIELD COY. R.E.	
	13/1/17		Company engaged in clean river inspection rough fabric and type inspection huts. Afternoon recreation	JM
	14/1/17		[Sunday] Inspection Parade on 13/1/17 2nd Cpl. Lyngoe 1st Cpl. Sergt. Eason R awarded bar to M.M.	JM
	15/1/17		Company inspected in erecting Nissen Huts. Afternoon recreation	JM
	16/1/17		Company engaged erecting Nissen Huts and in instruction on Rash Pipe Plant. Afternoon recreation	JM
	17/1/17		2nd Lt. Robertshaw admitted to Hospital (sick) Company engaged as on 16th & 17th	JM
	18/1/17			JM
	19/1/17		Company engaged in erecting Nissen Huts and instruction on Rash Pipe Plant. No 1 Section left for OUEN for VAUCHELLES.	JM
	20/1/17			JM
	21/1/17		Company engaged in Rifle scoring and testing of ammunition on Rash Pipe Plant. Remain inspection Reveille weather. Afternoon shorts.	JM
	22/1/17		Church Parade. Inspection of Billets.	JM
	23/1/17		Company engaged Company talk & one of Rash Pipe Plant. Afternoon Rifle testing.	JM

Army Form C. 2118.

WAR DIARY
or
INTELLIGENCE SUMMARY

(Erase heading not required.)

JANUARY 1917

Place	Date	Hour	Summary of Events and Information	Remarks and references to Appendices
			CHESHIRE FIELD COY. R.E.	
	23/1/16		Company now engaged in Company drill exercises on ease of hand rope bleach outdoor, training of stray periods, tunneled section fatigue, decorating an Aerodrome.	
	24/1/16		Company engaged in stove checks drill, saluting of arms, instruction in use of Pratt Rifle Grant- and anti gas drill. Afternoon sports.	
	25/1/16		Company engaged in close order inspection, Company drill, instruction in use of Pratt Rifle Grant, handling of Tools, throwing of milk in use of hostile parties. Afternoon sports	
	26/1/17		Company engaged in Company drill and route march.	
	27/1/17		In accordance with orders received from B.H.Q. 3rd Division Coy engaged in finding attention trenching wagon for move ahead for 28.1.17.	
	28/1/17		Company on zoute for AUTHIEULE. No 1 Section remained attached there place]	
	29/1/17		Company continued march to BEAUVOIR remaining there tonight	
	30/1/17		Company continued march to WIGNACOURT, remaining there in night	
	31/1/17		Company continued march to MARQUAY remaining one night	

John Standard
Capt RE
31/1/17

WAR DIARY or INTELLIGENCE SUMMARY

Army Form C. 2118.

W25 SHEET No 1.
1st February 1917

Place	Date	Hour	Summary of Events and Information	Remarks and references to Appendices
	1/2/17		450th CHESHIRE FIELD COY. R.E. Strength of Company checked by O.C. 39th Div Field Coy. Company defended march from MARQUAY to VILLERS-SIRE-SIMON. Company remained at VILLERS-SIRE-SIMON resting. Inspection of harness, arms and kit held.	JMc
	2/2/17		Company remained by route march to ARRAS less transport which proceeded to DUISANS.	JMc
	3/2/17		Company engaged in clearing and reforming billets in ARRAS.	JMc
	4/2/17		Company engaged on the following work. One section under Major Nelmes to ARRAS Montgomery and Lieut Pollard Rue de Temple Brigade HQ B.M.W.B. S.29.c & 7. One section under Lieut. Moshin Emplacements G.23. 7kD. 130.4.5c. One section constructing small dug outs for Battalion Head Quarters in Rue de Sévigné off ICELAND TRENCH S.35. A.6.8. One section continued with improvements of billets & improved Infantry Front. Returns have repaired the R12th Division Signal Cable on three plate.	JMc

2449 Wt. W14957/M90 750,000 1/16 J.B.C. & A. Forms/C.2118/12.

Army Form C. 2118.

SHEET No 2
FEBRUARY 1917.

WAR DIARY
or
INTELLIGENCE SUMMARY

(Erase heading not required.)

Instructions regarding War Diaries and Intelligence Summaries are contained in F. S. Regs., Part II. and the Staff Manual respectively. Title Pages will be prepared in manuscript.

Place	Date	Hour	Summary of Events and Information	Remarks and references to Appendices
	6/2/17		NORTONCHIRE FIELD COY. R.E.	
	7/2/17		Took over from an officer relieved by this Company of the Foresters on the 5/2/17. Saw hurdle and hurdle stakes sent from the 90th Field Company R.E. Interior of this RUE DE L'ANCIENT RIVAGE ARRAS G.22.a.4.4. One section employed in putting and clearing of Horse hides and repairing dug-outs at HOUSES.	JM
	13/2/17		On 13/2/17 took over number 6 R.E. of 31st Division work decided to undertake work in dug-outs front trenches and in School RUE DE TEMPLE. A new trench having been shown Company employed as follows: two sections on Revetment off ICELAND STREET, one section employed and on Trench Mortar Emplacements, Loopers in Parapets along the Front line and everything except the Engine in our Full Equipment employed as follows: two sections continued work on	JM
	14/2/17		Dug-outs in Meaulen place off ICELAND Road and another work on French Tunnel Explanations to one section employed Anew at R.E. through which were formed near the Gaol Saloon RUE DE TEMPLE.	JM
	15/2/17			JM

WAR DIARY / INTELLIGENCE SUMMARY

Army Form C. 2118.

Sheet No. 3
FEBRUARY 1917

430th CHESHIRE FIELD COY. R.E.

Company employed as follows. (Return continued work on dug-outs in Reserve Line, one section continued work on Tunnel Barrier Emplacements. One section used half-company work on burial dug-out in Tunnel at LAWRENCE STREET for Brigade Headquarters. Half section erecting nets and RE dumps. J Ryder & sub sections of mounted sappers and R.E workshop.

Working. Men above the Company were engaged on the following work (with the exception of the 27/2/17 when in accordance with Orders received from I Bde 3rd Return dated 25.2.17. As R.E. bent Employment). One section continued work on Tunnel Barrier Emplacements. One section employed work on dug-outs in Reserve Line. One section continued work on dug-out for Brigade Head Quarters in Tunnel at LAWRENCE STREET. One section half-company burial dug-out for Battalion Head quarters in Tunnel at Junction of ICELAND STREET and SUPPORT LINE, and continued work this month.

John Russell Major R.E.
O.C. 430th Cheshire Field Coy R.E.
28.2.17

Army Form C. 2118.

SHEET. No. 1

MARCH. 1917

Vol 26

WAR DIARY
or
INTELLIGENCE SUMMARY
(Erase heading not required.)

Place	Date	Hour	Summary of Events and Information	Remarks and references to Appendices
	1/3/17 to 28/3/17		438th (CHESHIRE) FIELD COY. R.E. The Company was employed during March chiefly on the following work. One section in construction of the Brigade Head Quarters, Dugout in LAURENCE AVENUE on section on Battalion Head Quarters. Dug-out and a TUNNEL at the junction of ICELAND STREET and the Vineyard Line. One section in Battalion Trench Mortar Emplacements to the accommodation of heavy Trench Mortars for Trench Mortar Battery. One section in the Tunnel near NINETEENTH STREET. Some have been being permanently employed at the R.E. Workshops in ZIRAS and have been on the R.E. dump near Pt. 91.26. SCHOOL RUE DE TEMPLE. One N.C.O. and 3 other ranks kept continuous watch on the Enemy together between Vpt. 18 & 19. One section was employed in improving small approach to M SAUVEUR TUNNEL for the I.T. the remaining sections were	MM MM
	22/3/17 to 29/3/17			
	30/3/17			MM

Army Form C. 2118.

SHEET No 2
MARCH 1917

WAR DIARY
or
INTELLIGENCE SUMMARY

(Erase heading not required.)

Instructions regarding War Diaries and Intelligence Summaries are contained in F. S. Regs., Part II. and the Staff Manual respectively. Title Pages will be prepared in manuscript.

Place	Date	Hour	Summary of Events and Information	Remarks and references to Appendices
	29/3/17 to 31/3/17		436th (CHESHIRE) FIELD COY. R.E. Employed in charging and refilling for establishment for Stokes mortar time of trip equipment and ammunition	JMR
	3/3/17		CASUALTIES 2nd LIEUTENANT H.T.F. GOURLEY wounded One other rank missing from the 22/3/17	

John Maud Knyfer R.E.
O.C. 436th Cheshire Field Coy R.E.

Army Form C. 2118.

WAR DIARY
or
INTELLIGENCE SUMMARY.
(Erase heading not required.)

488th (CHESHIRE) FIELD COMPANY, R.E.

APRIL 1917   SHEET No 1

Instructions regarding War Diaries and Intelligence Summaries are contained in F. S. Regs., Part II. and the Staff Manual respectively. Title pages will be prepared in manuscript.

Place	Date	Hour	Summary of Events and Information	Remarks and references to Appendices
	1/4/17		One section of the Company were employed in repairing the 3rd Division Heavy Trench Mortar Battery in consolidating a tunnel to one of the Gun positions near IMPERIAL STREET TRENCH. The remainder of this section in forming Gun Blinkings of pillars occupied by the 5th Infantry Brigade in the RUE DE TEMPLE and RUE DE RITZ.	JW
	2/4/17		One section of the Company engaged in sinking a northern recess from LAURENCE AVENUE One section Infantry Brigade Bomb Head Quarters in LAURENCE AVENUE One section creating shelters & dumps and made for a well at S.20.c.6.6. Another one working on repair of Dugout in IODINE STREET remainder of the Company employed in fatigues &c & trench warfare Infantry of 8th Brigade on sundry Jobs between the Town of the RUE DE RITZ.	JW
	3/4/17		The Company were employed as on the 2/4/17. The Company moved their Billets and were accommodated in cellars in the RUE CAPUCINE and BOULEVARD CARNOT ARRAS.	JW
	4/4/17 5/4/17 6/4/17 7/4/17 8/4/17		The Company were mostly employed during these days. One section being attached to a division of Pioneer Corps engaged in repairs to roads in the neighbourhood of the station turned out on the 5th to allow detachments into the FAUBIMONT GATE and PLACE VICTOR HUGO.	JW

Army Form C. 2118.

WAR DIARY
or
INTELLIGENCE SUMMARY.
(Erase heading not required.)

APRIL 1917. SHEET No 2.

493RD (CHECKED) FIELD COMPANY, R.E.

Place	Date	Hour	Summary of Events and Information	Remarks and references to Appendices
	9/4/17		The Company first heard in rather general characters opened of the enemy carried out by the Front, and I had having with the object of capturing the defensive system running from ARRAS to CAMBRAI. The Company were employed on the front of the 3rd Division. The Southern Boundary of this Division being S.35.c.8.0. G.36.c.2.7. M.6.c.4.5. thence along the road G.M.7.a.5.8.N d.9.5. thence a straight line to the German Front System the Southern known along being S.30.c.8.2. G.30.d.2½.2. H.31.a.1.6½. H.31.a.4.4. thence along the road to H.31.d.a.5.9½ – N.3.d.4½.7. thence a straight line to the German 3rd System. The 3rd Divisions objectives were the following:– 1st Objective (Black Line) the German Front System viz:– G.1. G.36.c.9.4. G.36.c.5.0. G.36.d.P.9. Eastern edge DEVILS WOOD 2nd Objective (Blue Line) the German second system of Trenches NOISY REDOUBT. Tunnel N.1.d.3.0. N.1.d.2.3. N.1.b.9.4. N.1.a.9½.4. N.1.B.1.6. H.31.d.6.4. H.31.d.9.4. H.32.c.1.7. 3rd Objective (Brown Line) the German second system of trenches HANCOURT – FEUCHY LINE including the Bavarian & Bavarian Redoubts. MAP REFERENCE TILLOY 1:10000. The 1st Objective was allotted to the 76th Infantry Brigade the second to the 9th Infantry Brigade, and the third to the 8th Infantry Brigade	JMC

Army Form C. 2118.

WAR DIARY
or
INTELLIGENCE SUMMARY.
(Erase heading not required.)

APRIL 1917 SHEET No 3

488TH (CHESHIRE) FIELD COMPANY, R.E.

Place	Date	Hour	Summary of Events and Information	Remarks and references to Appendices
	9/4/17		The Head Quarters of the Company during operations were at 21 RUE DES CAPUCINS, ARRAS. Sections 1 and 3 were in DIVISIONAL Reserve under the Orders of the C.R.E. 3rd Francaise Sections 2 & 4 were attached to the 8th Infantry Brigade and came under the Orders of the G.O.C. of that Brigade. On the morning of the 9th the whole Company were on their Billets in cellars on the RUE DES CAPUCINS and BOULEVARD CARNOT, ARRAS. The Officer Commanding was at the Battle Head Quarters of the 8th Infantry Brigade h carrying party of 90 men of the 1st Battalion Royal Scots Fusiliers were at the F.P.O. 140 were attached to the Company for operations and one Section was accommodated in the INFANTRY BARRACKS, ARRAS. At 11 AM on this date Orders were received from the G.O.C. 8th Infantry Brigade to bring up the carrying party and Orders were issued accordingly this party reported at the Brigade Advanced Headquarters at 12 noon the Set. Given an hour's rest ate out 12 noon and were mobilised to march forward as far as forwardthe trenches from the 3rd Objective northwest lifting around up in the fighting.	JMW

WAR DIARY or INTELLIGENCE SUMMARY

Army Form C. 2118.

APRIL 1917
SHEET No 4

48TH (?) FIELD COMPANY, R.E.

Place	Date	Hour	Summary of Events and Information	Remarks and references to Appendices
	9/4/17		At 2 P.M. Orders were received to move up positions 2 and 4 to the 8th Infantry Brigade Head Quarters on the old German front line and there awaiting reported there at 3.45 P.M. calling on the way at the R.E. Dump for stores. At 6.55 P.M. orders were received from the C.R.E. to move section No 3 forward on the ARTILLERY ROAD along the Divisional South Boundary and this section proceeded there at 7.10 P.M. All attacks by the 8th Infantry Brigade made this day on the third objective failed and at 10-15 P.M. it was decided to consolidate on the new line attempts made to outflank Hickson's 2·4 and 87 field company ephemeral there to outflank Hickson 2·4 and 87 field company all them. Bullets coming about 12·30 P.M. together with the company parts.	AM
	1/4/17		At 5·30 A.M. sections 2·4 together with the company forty proceeded to the 8th Infantry Brigade Advance Head Quarters. At 10·15 P.M. orders were received that the 3rd Objective had been captured and at 1·45 P.M. orders were received to move the company forty and sections 2·4 forward for the purpose of consolidation	AM

Army Form C. 2118

APRIL 1917
SHEET No 5

WAR DIARY
or
INTELLIGENCE SUMMARY
(Erase heading not required.)

Place	Date	Hour	Summary of Events and Information	Remarks and references to Appendices
	10/4/17		438th (CHESHIRE) FIELD COY. R.E. The unexploded mine and another strong points at N11 a 7 and N10 a 3.9. At 2.30 P.M. Orders were received from the C.R.E. to withdraw Nº 2 and Nº 3 sections to a camp to be pitched on the ARTILLERY ROAD and this section proceeded there at 2-30 P.M. At 3.45. P.M. Further orders were received from the C.R.E. instructing that sections 2 and 4 would also the regiment be moved as the attack fixed on the 11/4/17. The O.C. Company obtained permission from the G.O.C. 98th Infantry Brigade to withdraw these two sections and at once proceeded to the Brown Line and instructed the Officers in charge of sections there sections as there was great insufficiency returned to camp the Infantry for sundry complete at 9.30 P.M. Sections 2 & 4 were withdrawn and returned to their Battn. hq. at 12-30 A.M. on the 11.4.17. Section 3 returned to Billets at 5 P.M on the 10.4.17 and sixteen 1 at 8 P.M on the same date. The working party returned to their Billets at 12 midnight on the 10.4.17	

Army Form C. 2118.

WAR DIARY
or
INTELLIGENCE SUMMARY
(Erase heading not required.)

APRIL 1917
SHEET No 6

Instructions regarding War Diaries and Intelligence Summaries are contained in F. S. Regs., Part II. and the Staff Manual respectively. Title Pages will be prepared in manuscript.

Place	Date	Hour	Summary of Events and Information	Remarks and references to Appendices
	1/4/17		438th (CHESHIRE) FIELD COY. R.E.	
	12/4/17		During this period the whole of the 4 sections of the Company were employed under orders of the C.R.E. 3rd Division on repair of the ARTILLERY ROAD	JMc
	13/4/17			
	14/4/17		The 3rd Divison proceeded on the line and the Company commenced to Billets. Inspection of Foot Rifles Rations were carried out.	
	15/4/17			
	16/4/17			
	17/4/17		Inspection of Arms and Equipment carried out.	
	18/4/17		Church Pde at Pontoons and Pitcher Trestles on the afternoon of the 17th. Sections one and two employed in removing and repairing Horse Troughs on the 15th and 18th.	JMc
	19/4/17			
	20/4/17		Section the Company were standing by marching for orders.	
	21/4/17		The Company Hd Head Quarters and details moved forward in accordance with Orders from C.R.E. 3rd Division and are	JMc
	22/4/17		billeted in old German lines in THE STRING of the HARP at N.1.c64.	
	23/4/17		TILLOY SHEET 51.NW.1. The Company remained there in accordance with orders received from S.O.C. 76th Infantry Brigade with the exception of the 4 sections which have been employed laboring Labor with AUSHARLAMES THE MONCHY.	JMc

2449 Wt. W14957/M90 750,000 1/16 J.B.C. & A. Forms/C.2118/12.

Army Form C. 2118.

APRIL 1917
Sheet No 7.

488th (CHESHIRE) FIELD COMPANY, R.E.

WAR DIARY
or
INTELLIGENCE SUMMARY.
(Erase heading not required.)

Instructions regarding War Diaries and Intelligence Summaries are contained in F.S. Regs., Part II. and the Staff Manual respectively. Title pages will be prepared in manuscript.

Place	Date	Hour	Summary of Events and Information	Remarks and references to Appendices
	25/4/17		The Company were engaged in wiring the line of trenches of MONCHY starting at point O.7.b.5.9. The Monchfeld section on trench 9/0 connected on to HUSSAR LANE for the first time	MM
	26/4/17			
	27/4/17		The Company were wiring	
	28/4/17		Sections 1 & 5 were engaged in wiring the new defensive line of MONCHY Sections 2 & 4 men carried carrying material to somewhere of wiring	MM
	29/4/17		Sections 2 & 4 were employed wiring in front of somewhere 7 and it was necessary for my Sections it 3 were wiring	MM

Casualties.

2 Lieut. H. J. A. MANNING.
Wounded at duty.
Other Ranks 7.
Killed 1.

2.4.17 7th H.Q. N.F. Jackson wounded Hospital Field Hospital
8.4.17 7th W.S.q. B. Kelly " "
9.4.17 7th S.F. Jackson returned from duty — from 5-59 R.F.A   "
29.4.17 7th H.A. Breckluck to Hospital Field
29.4.17 7th   "   to Hospital Field

MM

A5831   Wt. W4973/M687 750,000 8/16 D. D. & L. Ltd. Forms/C.2118/13.

Army Form C. 2118.

WAR DIARY
INTELLIGENCE SUMMARY.
(Erase heading not required.)

MAY 1917 SHEET N°1.
Vol 28

458th (Che???) Field Company, R.E.

Place	Date	Hour	Summary of Events and Information	Remarks and references to Appendices
	1/5/17		N°.1 Section were employed in making out with what the front overland route from N.3.R.8.6 to junction of HUSSAR and BRAYSOENZANES with MONCHY. 6 men of this section are making O.P. near HUSSAR LANE and am??? ??? section in improving 57th Brigade Battle Headquarters. The remainder of the Company were resting.	JM
	2/5/17		Company received orders from 3rd Division to ??? from the line of the HARP via TILLOY to line HENGIST TRENCH SOUTH of the CAMBRAI ROAD. By 9 P.M. Men were carried out and the Company obtained type to consolidate gains in an attack to the south on the morrow. Possible on the following day. Transport was engaged in carrying up materials. Bridges to HUSSAR LANE.	9PM
	3/5/17		The whole company was engaged in moving NE edge of WOOD E.9. MONCHY in front of recent enemy from O.I.B.S.4.H.O.I.a.b.7. Transport in taking ??? enemy material to HUSSAR LANE.	10PM
	4/5/17		Company and Transport employed as on 3rd.	9PM
	5/5/17		Company employed on H.Q. ????	9PM
	6/5/17		????	9PM
	7/5/17		????	9PM

Army Form C. 2118.

WAR DIARY
INTELLIGENCE SUMMARY
(Erase heading not required.)

438TH (CHESHIRE) FIELD COMPANY, R.E.

MAY 1917 Sheet No 2

Place	Date	Hour	Summary of Events and Information	Remarks and references to Appendices
	8/5/17		Company employed with working parties supplied by the 8th Infantry Brigade in constructing and improving tramways in sector Trench TINE LANE which had been commenced from EAST and GRAPE TRENCHES MONCHY. Tramway went up to old German trench at No 5 2'6". Transport engaged in taking up trench boards & slump in HUSSAR LANE.	JM
	9/5/17 10/5/17 11/5/17 12/5/17 13/5/17		As there respective dates the Company was employed as in the my/pliof: 8/5/17.	JM
	14/5/17		The Division was relieved and the Company proceeded under orders of the 8th Brigade to DAINVILLE. Left Line at 8.30 P.M. arrived Lower halt ARRAS at 9.30 P.M. left ARRAS 10.30 P.M arrived DAINVILLE 11.30 P.M.	JM
	15/5/17		Company working baths &c, thoroughly cleaning.	JM
	16/5/17		Company cleaning clothes arms kits &c further harness inspection and	JM

Army Form C. 2118.

WAR DIARY
INTELLIGENCE SUMMARY
(Erase heading not required.)

438TH (CHESHIRE) FIELD COMPANY, R.E.

MAY 1917 Sheet No 3

Place	Date	Hour	Summary of Events and Information	Remarks and references to Appendices
	17/5/17		The Company remained resting at DAINVILLE	JW
	18/5/17		The Company proceeded by rail road to WANQUETIN leaving DAINVILLE at 8.45 A.M. and arriving at noon and took one week of refresher training general day experience of reconnoitring charge the Company were made under of the C.E. XVIII Corps.	JW
	19/5/17 to 31/5/17		The Company continued the above work at WANQUETIN the following training was also carried out during this period Lewis Gun drill and handling of same, 10 hours Lecture on Railway Trestle Bridges and practical work of same 8 hours. Lectures and practical work of suspension 4 hours. Mounted section turned out on an average of 2 times per week when no work exactly should.	JW

Casualties
Wounded to Other Ranks.
28-5-17   II/W. H.J.A. BRADDOCK returned the Company from No.1 Officers Stationary Hospital.

John Edmund [Wragg?] M.C. RE
O.C. 438th Cheshire Field Company R.E.

Army Form C. 2118.

Vol 24

JUNE 1917. SHEET. No 1.

488th (WESSEX) FIELD COMPANY, R.E.

WAR DIARY or INTELLIGENCE SUMMARY.

(Erase heading not required.)

Place	Date	Hour	Summary of Events and Information	Remarks and references to Appendices
	1/6/17		The Company were engaged in repair of dwellings damaged by explosion.	JW
	2/6/17		The Company left WANQUETIN and proceed to line NORT. EAST of TILLOY	JW
LES MOFFLAINES	3/6/17		Two sections were employed on completion of Dug Out in strong point F	JW
	4/6/17 5/6/17		N.W. of MONCHY LE PREUX. One section on improving SNAFFLE TRENCH in front of MONCHY. One section on improving shelters in company front.	JW
	6/6/17		One section engaged on dug out as above, two sections working on SNAFFLE TR.	JW
	7/6/17 8/6/17 9/6/17		Two sections engaged in work on SNAFFLE TRENCH one section on dug out as above, one section on dug out at O 8 a 7.6.	JW
	10/6/17 11/6/17 12/6/17 13/6/17 14/6/17			
	15/6/17		Took handed over to 529th EAST RIDING FIELD COMPANY R.E. and proceeded to BILLETS in ARRAS.	JW

WAR DIARY
INTELLIGENCE SUMMARY

Army Form C. 2118.
SHEET No 2
JUNE 1917

Place	Date	Hour	Summary of Events and Information	Remarks and references to Appendices
	19/6/17		Company proceeded by route march to HABARCQ and encamped there for one night.	MR
	20/6/17		Company proceeded by route march to BERLENCOURT.	MR
	21/6/17		Company arrived at BERLENCOURT. setting up clothing and equipment, inspections held.	MR
	22/6/17		Company at BERLENCOURT. Commenced harness throughting of overhead water drill.	MR
	22/6/17			
	23/6/17		Company at BERLENCOURT training. Close order drill, musketry instruction, knots and lashings, pontooning.	JhG
	24/6/17		Company at BERLENCOURT Church parade. Lecture by M.O. "First Aid"	JhG
	25/6/17		do 3 sections training. Close order drill, musketry instruction, pontooning, physical drill.	JhG
	26/6/17		do 3 sections musketry practice on range	JhG
	27/6/17		do 1 section. Erection of permanent bridge at WAMIN over la CANCHE Rivière	JhG
	28/6/17		Orders received that division would be transferred from VI Corps to I Corps. Company moved by road to MILLY with 8th Inf Bde – 8th Inf Bde O.O. No 47	JhG
	29/6/17		" (8oo transport) to DOULLENS by train to ACHIET LE GRAND, by road to GOMIECOURT – 8th Inf Bde O.O. No 48 Transport by road to GOMIECOURT.	JhG

Army Form C. 2118.
SHEET No 3

WAR DIARY
INTELLIGENCE SUMMARY
(Erase heading not required.)

438TH (CHESHIRE) FIELD COMPANY, R.E.

JUNE 1917

Instructions regarding War Diaries and Intelligence Summaries are contained in F.S. Regs., Part II. and the Staff Manual respectively. Title pages will be prepared in manuscript.

Place	Date	Hour	Summary of Events and Information	Remarks and references to Appendices
	30/5/17		Coy. moved by road to LEBUCQUIERE – 8th Inf. Bde O.O. No. 49. and took over billets from 474th (S.M.) Fld. Co. R.E. Work in left Brigade sector was taken over from 475th (S.M.) Fld Co.R.E. and a/oc. and 3 officers reconnoitred a forward area with a/oc. 475th Fld Co. R.E.	JMcG.
			CASUALTIES	
			Killed 1. O.R.	
			Wounded 6. O.R. (one since died)	
	10/6/17		IIW H.A. BRADDOCK to hospital sick	JMcG.
	16/6/17		IIW C.G. FUNNELL joined from 579th (S.R.) Field Co R.E. and rejoined Hd company 23/6/17	
	19/6/17		IIW J.J. FISHER joined unit from Base.	JMcG.
	23/6/17		IIW E.T. COTTERELL " from 445th (Welsh Reserve) Fld Co R.E.	JMcG.
			IIW G.A. MANNING awarded M.C. authority 3rd Divn R.O. 15/6/17	JMcG.

JMcGill
Mr. Capt. R.E. (T)
a/oc. 438th (Ches) Field Co. R.E.

Army Form C. 2118.

SHEET 1.

Vol. 30 JULY 1917

438TH (CHESHIRE) FIELD COMPANY, R.E.

WAR DIARY
or
INTELLIGENCE SUMMARY.
(Erase heading not required.)

Instructions regarding War Diaries and Intelligence Summaries are contained in F. S. Regs., Part II. and the Staff Manual respectively. Title pages will be prepared in manuscript.

Place	Date	Hour	Summary of Events and Information	Remarks and references to Appendices
LOUVERVAL	1/7/17		Started work in LOUVERVAL SECTION, RIGHT SECTOR, IV Corps Area. 1 Section on culvert J10a.7-6 Sh.57c, 1 off. 20r. with inf. party 190 Inf. Bde on improving posts 30 and 31. LOUVERVAL, DOIGNIES, HERMIES line. Party 70r. on well at J10a.8-9. 3off. 6 NCOs reconnoitring forward area.	JMcG
	2/7/17		1 section on culvert J10a.7-6. Party on well J10a.8-9. Remainder improving billets	JMcG
	3/7/17		1 section on culvert J10a.7-6 (completed). 1 section on improving posts No 31 with inf. party of 8th Inf. Bde. Party on well at J10a.8-9.	JMcG
	4/7/17		1 section on posts 31, 32, 33 and 34 with inf. party 8th Inf. Bde. Party on well at J10a.8-9. 1 off. reconnoitring other sites for wells, 1off. reconnoitring dugouts.	JMcG
	5/7/17		1 section on posts 31, 33 and 34 with inf. party 8th Inf. Bde. 1 section on	JMcG
	6/7/17		posts 22 and 24. improving trenches and completing dugouts.	JMcG
	7/7/17		1 section working on posts 35 + 36 LOUVERAL HERMIES LINE. One section on posts 21, 22 + 24. on this line. one section working on Brigade and Company head quarters.	JMcG

Army Form C. 2118.

WAR DIARY
INTELLIGENCE SUMMARY

(Erase heading not required.)

July 1917 SHEET 2

438th (CHESHIRE) FIELD COMPANY, R.E.

Place	Date	Hour	Summary of Events and Information	Remarks and references to Appendices
	8/7/17		Two sections employed on dug outs and entrance trench to posts 22.20 & 26. HERMIES LOUVERAL LINE. 12 Sun on Hell at LOUVERAL.	JM
	9/7/17 10/7/17		Two sections employed as above. 6 Sun on Hell at LOUVERAL and 6 Sun on wiring Dan Hell at Mc Millan's C.S.O. C.77.	JM
	11/7/17		Two sections employed on Posts 22.20 & 25. 33 v 34 (with infantry parties). HERMIES LOUVERAL LINE. Party wiring LOUVERAL defences. Party on road CAMBRAI BAPUME Road. Party sinking a Cambrai shaft at LOUVERAL at I 15 a 9.8. Posts on the Hells as above.	JM
	12/7/17 13/7/17 14/7/17 15/7/17 16/7/17 17/7/17		Company employed as above and in addition one further post on a communication trench from the sunken [?] to post L.32.	JM
	18/7/17		Company continued work on posts Hell at LOUVERAL and on post 22. 23. 29. 31. 32. 33. 34 35 36 and on post at CAMBRAI- BAPUME ROAD and continued at J 10 a 9.8. The following post work was taken in hand namely posts in Reserve Line in front of LOUVERAL and posts in hamlet of DOIGNIES, construction of a trench across the LEBUCQUIERE - HERMIES clay railway track and a Bun Runner [?] trench from J 10 6 2.6 South of the CAMBRAI ROAD to post L.13.	JM

Army Form C. 2118.

WAR DIARY
INTELLIGENCE SUMMARY
(Erase heading not required.)

July 1917 SHEET 3

488TH COMBINED FIELD COMPANY, R.E.

Instructions regarding War Diaries and Intelligence Summaries are contained in F.S. Regs., Part II. and the Staff Manual respectively. Title pages will be prepared in manuscript.

Place	Date	Hour	Summary of Events and Information	Remarks and references to Appendices
	19/7/17 to 30/7/17		The Company were engaged in work now on the 18th the party working on the half at LOUVERAL completed their work on the 25th and joined the party raising the LOUVERAL defences	AW
	30/7/17		The Company were engaged as now on the 11th. The party working on the C.T. to front L.13 completed the portion of the trench dug and finished the party commenced work on a new communication trench to front L.1. South of BOURSIES.	AW

CASUALTIES

2nd Lieutenant H.J.F GOURLEY attached to C.R.E. 3rd Division (acting)

One other O.R. wounded (at duty)

J.H. Phenrel Major R.E.
O.C. 488th Field Coy.
1.8.17.

Army Form C. 2118.

WAR DIARY
INTELLIGENCE SUMMARY.
(Erase heading not required.)

AUGUST 1917. Sheet No. 1.

Place	Date	Hour	Summary of Events and Information	Remarks and references to Appendices
LEBUCQUIERE	1/8/17		The Company was engaged in the following work with Infantry Working Parties. Repairing and resetting posts No. 22, 24 & 25 LOUVERVAL. Completed chain at Redoubt at LOUVERVAL. Completed chain communication Fence from J.10.c.2.6. to point L.13. with chain and check bands. Wiring defences of LOUVERVAL VILLAGE and Reference VELU-BEAUMETZ ROAD and CAMBRAI ROAD and obey ent at J.17.a.6.6. Pudn on points 22, 24, 25 now completed.	MM
"	2/8/17		The Company were engaged on the 1/8/17 and commenced a new Communication Trench from J.C.6.2. to point L.1. and when Trench obey out at point 26.	MM
"	3/8/17		The Company were engaged on the 2/8/17 and also commenced a Trench obey cent and Junction Gear Emplacement at J.4.d.7.5.	MM
"	11/8/17 to 11/8/17		The Company were engaged on from the 3rd to 11th August and also on extending Tunnel at BEAUMETZ	MM
"	12/8/17		The company continued work as on the 12/7/17 but in Tunnel at BEAUMETZ was completed and other trench obey cent at J.4.d.7.5.	MM
"	12/8/17 to 16/8/17			MM
"	17/8/17		The company continued work as on the 16/8/17 and commenced work on Trench obey out at J.17.a.5.6. and a Communication Trench from Junction Pent at K.7.c.9.3. to point K.7.2. at K.7. d.3.5.	MM

Army Form C. 2118.

WAR DIARY
INTELLIGENCE SUMMARY.
(Erase heading not required.)

Instructions regarding War Diaries and Intelligence Summaries are contained in F. S. Regs., Part II. and the Staff Manual respectively. Title pages will be prepared in manuscript.

438TH (CHESHIRE) FIELD COMPANY R.E.

AUGUST 1917 Sheet No 2

Place	Date	Hour	Summary of Events and Information	Remarks and references to Appendices
LEBUCQUIERE	10/8/17 to 29/8/17		The Company continued work as on the 17/8/17 and completed the Communication trench from Junction Road at K.7c.9.3 to forward K.7.2 on the 29th August	JM
	30/8/17 to 31/8/17		The Company commenced work as on the 29/8/17 and also commenced sunken access in VELU-BEAUMETZ ROAD.	JM
			Casualties	
			6.8.17 One O.R.	JM
			16.8.17 One O.R.	JM

John Phund Major R.E.
O.C. 438 Cheshire Field Coy R.E.
31.8.17.

Army Form C. 2118.

Vol 3 ²⁄₁₉₁₇
SEPTEMBER SHEET No 1.

WAR DIARY

INTELLIGENCE SUMMARY
(Erase heading not required.)

Instructions regarding War Diaries and Intelligence Summaries are contained in F. S. Regs., Part II. and the Staff Manual respectively. Title pages will be prepared in manuscript.

Place	Date	Hour	Summary of Events and Information	Remarks and references to Appendices
	1/9/17 to 4/9/17		The Company was at LEBUCQUIERE and engaged in the following work hand dug out at J.17 a.5.6 dug out to J. and 26 LOUVERVAL LINE enemy between posts 25 & 28 LOUVERVAL LINE and renewing old gun pits to the C.M. work was handed over to the 513th Field Company R.E.	JM
	5/9/17		The Company proceeded by Route March to LITTLEWOOD CAMP YPRES	JM
	6/9/17 to 17/9/17		The Company remained at LITTLEWOOD CAMP during this period and the following training was carried out. Musketry two stages (entering 1 use of Holcter Trestle, two stages refue' running two stage smoking barbwire & use of spare stays, erection of Knieff steel trestles and close wire cleats, handling of arms, Use of explosives one day.	JM
	18/9/17		The Company marched to PAPUME and entrained for PROVEN	JM
	19/9/17		The Company arrived at PROVEN and detrained and proceed by Route March to R. billets in VLAMERTINGHE.	JM
	20/9/17		Company engaged in Company fatigues.	JM

Army Form C. 2118.

WAR DIARY
INTELLIGENCE SUMMARY
(Erase heading not required.)

288th (CHESHIRE) FIELD COMPANY, R.E.

1917 SEPTEMBER SHEET No 2

Instructions regarding War Diaries and Intelligence Summaries are contained in F. S. Regs., Part II. and the Staff Manual respectively. Title pages will be prepared in manuscript.

Place	Date	Hour	Summary of Events and Information	Remarks and references to Appendices
	21st 22nd		The Company was engaged in erecting NISSEN HUTS at Hosfield Camp No 2 Area VLAMERTINGHE	AM
	23rd		The Company proceeded by & route march to Hellebeken YPRES and 3 sections employed in work on an emergency Pro TANKS and D26R53.3 one pr from an opening road at C.30.8	AM
	24th 25th		Two sections continued work on TANK crossing and two others on tracks "H" & "K" to front line	AM
	26th 27th 28th		Two sections were specially attached to the 5th Infantry Brigade for the return and to construct three strong points one of these was constructed. Two sections under the orders of the 6 R.E. 3rd Division were employed on constructing and section of H & K Tracks to the front line.	AM
	29th 30th		The Company was employed with one Coys of Pioneers in constructing Tracks and Tramways near the ZONNEBEKE	AM

Army Form C. 2118.

WAR DIARY

INTELLIGENCE SUMMARY

(Erase heading not required.)

498th (Chesire) FIELD COMPANY, R.E.

SEPTEMBER 1917 (1455) pg 3

Instructions regarding War Diaries and Intelligence Summaries are contained in F. S. Regs., Part II. and the Staff Manual respectively. Title pages will be prepared in manuscript.

Place	Date	Hour	Summary of Events and Information	Remarks and references to Appendices
			Casualties	
	19th		Lieut. P. BACK. R.M.C. Wounded. H.E. Shell fire (attached.)	M.
	24th		One O.R. Wounded. VLAMERTINGHE (activity.) Explosion of an ammunition dump at	M.
	26th		Lt. H. SAMANNING. Killed. MILL COTTAGE. Enemy in the Sallet.	M.
			10 O.R. Wounded. Enemy Shrapnel and H.E. fire.	M.
	30th		3 O.R. Killed. } Enemy Aeroplane Bombs.	M.
			8 O.R. Wounded. }	M.

John Plunkett Inger (?)
R.E. M.
O.C. 498th Cheshire Field Coy.
30.9.17

Army Form C. 2118.

WAR DIARY
or
INTELLIGENCE SUMMARY

(Erase heading not required.)

438 2nd CHSHEET No. 1.
OCTOBER 1917
JM 33

Place	Date	Hour	Summary of Events and Information	Remarks and references to Appendices
			438th (CHESHIRE) FIELD COY. R.E.	
	1/10/17	—	The dismounted portion of the Company moved from their billets in YPRES by route march and joined the mounted section at BRANDHOEK, remaining there that night in hutted camp.	JM
	2/10/17		The dismounted portion of the Company proceeded by train to WINNEZEELE and was billeted. The mounted section proceeded by road to the same destination.	JM
	3/10/17		The Company remained at WINNEZEELE and paraded with the 6th Infantry Brigade for inspection by the G.O.C. 3rd Division.	JM
	4/10/17		The Company proceeded by route march to RENESCURE and were billeted.	JM
	5/10/17		The Company proceeded by route march to ST. OMER and entrained for BAPAUME.	JM
	6/10/17		The Company detrained at BAPAUME and proceeded to hutted camp at BEAULENCOURT.	JM
	7/10/17 to 10/10/17		The Company remained in camp at BEAULENCOURT and were employed in improving the camp and erecting a Y.M.C.A. Hut.	JM

2449 Wt. W14957/M90 750,000 1/16 J.B.C. & A. Forms/C.2118/12.

Army Form C. 2118.

SHEET No. 2.

OCTOBER 1917

WAR DIARY
or
INTELLIGENCE SUMMARY.
(Erase heading not required.)

Instructions regarding War Diaries and Intelligence Summaries are contained in F. S. Regs., Part II. and the Staff Manual respectively. Title pages will be prepared in manuscript.

Place	Date	Hour	Summary of Events and Information	Remarks and references to Appendices
	1/10/17		The Company proceeded by route march to Camp No. 12 BEUGNATRE and took over work from the 457th Field Company R.E.	JM
	12/10/17 to 21/10/17		Three sections of the Company were employed in building Battalion Billets at L'ABBAYE MORY. The remaining section was employed on R.E. dumps and workshops & camouflage on the MORY-ECOUST Rd. this hutto-work being completed on the 23rd. Putting up huts for 93rd Bathy at H.12 central for two companies and putting up of showers near Fossa huts.	JM
	22/10/17 to 30/10/17		One section was sent to ACHIET-LE-PETIT to work on huts there sections continued work on L'ABBAYE MORY and the remainder of the Company were employed as before.	JM
	31/10/17		The Company was employed as above and work was also commenced on a Gun Boot staging shed at FAVREUIL.	JM
			Casualties NIL.	M.

John Ahmad Mayor RE(T)
O.C. 438th Field Company
R.E.
7/11/17

Army Form C. 2118.

SHEET No 1
1917

WAR DIARY
INTELLIGENCE SUMMARY
(Erase heading not required.)

Instructions regarding War Diaries and Intelligence Summaries are contained in F.S. Regs., Part II. and the Staff Manual respectively. Title pages will be prepared in manuscript.

480th (Gleeshire) FIELD COMPANY R.E.

Vol 34 NOVEMBER

Place	Date	Hour	Summary of Events and Information	Remarks and references to Appendices
	6/11/17		The Company were engaged on erection of quarters for a Battalion at L'ABBAYE MORY. Sections 1, 2 & 4 and proportion of HQ echon proceeded to NOREUIL and took over billets and work on Right Bde Section from 3 Sections of 56th Field Co R.E. No 3 Section remained at MORY.	JHG JHG
	7/11/17		No 1 section on ILKLEY SUPPORT MECHING. No 2 Section in SHEFFIELD SUPPORT MECHING. No 4 section in LONDON SUPPORT, dubbing. Small parties on TANK NOREUIL ROAD, SIDNEY CROSS, Newport Half and Bec Bank Horne NOREUIL	JHG
	8/11/17		Do. Same as for 7th and in addition 2 parties on MG dugouts and two MG nests	JHG
	9/11/17		No 2 section changed from work on SHEFFIELD SUPPORT to TOWER TRENCH. Other work as for the 8th.	JHG
	10/11/17		No 1 section changed from work on ILKLEY SUPPORT to TANK AVENUE. Other work as for the 9th. Arriving on LONDON SUPPORT Completed.	JHG
	11/11/17		Do. for the 10th, with exception that section 4 worked on TANK AVE	JHG
	12/11/17		No 2 section stopped cleaning out dugouts in FRONT LINE, No 1 & 4 cleaning trench LONDON SUPPORT. No 4 section & No 3 section interchanged work and treats. No 3 proceeded from MORY to NOREUIL NO 4 from NOREUIL to MORY	JHG

Army Form C. 2118.

WAR DIARY
~~INTELLIGENCE SUMMARY.~~
(Erase heading not required.)

438TH (CHESHIRE) FIELD COMPANY, R.E.

NOVEMBER 1917 SHEET No 2

Place	Date	Hour	Summary of Events and Information	Remarks and references to Appendices
	13/11/17		No 1 Section continued a forward FRONT LINE from U 23 a.c. No 3 Section a forward FRONT LINE U 29.d. Moved billets north up to Bde 12 L.L.	
	14/11/17		Same as for 13th	
	15/11/17		"	
	16/11/17		Started fitting up Odr. Bde HQ NOREUIL	
	17/11/17		"	
	18/11/17		Cleaning trench line dugouts. Completed No 4 Section proceeded from Mory to NOREUIL	
	19/11/17		All work cancelled except MG dugouts & Bde HQ NOREUIL	
			Standing by. No 4 Section Camp under orders of GOC 8th Inf Bde	
	20/11/17		Major WARD returned from leave & resumed command. Co (less 1 section) Camp under orders of CRE 3rd Div. for work. Commenced work on heavy Ecoust Bullecourt Road	
	24/11/17		Work was continued on the Ecoust – Bullecourt Road. The Company rested and No 4 Section reserved from th. Burgade. One section engaged on repair on TANK AVENUE One section on Northern camp	
	28/11/17		at - MORY. NORTH and two sections on repair of NOREUIL-ECOUST ROAD	
	29/11/17			
	30/11/17			

Army Form C. 2118.

SHEET No 3.

NOVEMBER 1917

WAR DIARY
or
INTELLIGENCE SUMMARY

438th (CHESHIRE) FIELD COY. R.E.

(Erase heading not required.)

CASUALTIES

16/11/17. Lt. A.W. Davies left Unit for England.

29/11/17. One O.R. wounded.

RH.

RH.

John Stuart Knoyn

Capt RE

OC 438th Cheshire Field Coy RE

30th November 1917.

Army Form C. 2118.

DECEMBER 1917.
SHEET NO 1.

WAR DIARY
or
INTELLIGENCE SUMMARY.
(Erase heading not required.)

498TH (QUEENSLAND)
FIELD COMPANY, R.E.

Place	Date	Hour	Summary of Events and Information	Remarks and references to Appendices
	1/12/17 to 2/12/17		The Company have one section were employed on the MOEUVRES SECTOR. One section clearing trench and revetting JUNCTION OF TANK AVENUE and FRONT LINE. Two sections on cleaning trench from MOEUVRES ECOUST ROAD and widening of same. Section re-siting and improving Medical Camps at MORY NORTH.	M
	3/12/17 4/12/17		One section engaged on work on FRONT LINE in where two sections clearing and fitting & putting Duck Boards for from F.L. to front line between FOXTROT TRENCH and TANK AVENUE. also on revetment of dug outs N 23 and 144.	M
	5/12/17		The Company were employed as follows. One Section on revetment of trenches. One section on improvement of MORY NORTH CAMP.	M
	6/12/17		Three sections were engaged on revetting Support line between RAILWAY RESERVE and front N 29 d 5.7. and on LONDON SUPPORT - PUDSEY SUPPORT. One section making on MORY NORTH CAMP as above.	M
	7/12/17		One section engaged on revetment of the front and RAILWAY RESERVE one section improving Rail Head Line sidings on FOXTROT and TANK AVENUE one section on MORY NORTH CAMP an Engineers dug out No 9 in RAILWAY RESERVE.	M
	8/12/17 to 10/12/17		Two sections employed on Deep Dugout ROLLWAY RESERVE the west end left of SYDNEY AVENUE. One section employed at MORY NORTH R.E. work left of from same cleaning PUDSEY SUPPORT TRENCH.	M

Army Form C. 2118.

DECEMBER 1917.

SHEET N° 2

WAR DIARY
INTELLIGENCE SUMMARY.
(Erase heading not required.)

Instructions regarding War Diaries and Intelligence Summaries are contained in F. S. Regs., Part II. and the Staff Manual respectively. Title pages will be prepared in manuscript.

Place	Date	Hour	Summary of Events and Information	Remarks and references to Appendices
	11/4/17		One Section working at MORY NORTH CAMP on dugouts. Remaining 3 Sections were relieved in the line by the 5th P.W.V. Coy & R.E. and returned to their new Hut quarters at MO.12 Camp A.12.C.2.4.	WD
	12/4/17 13/4/17		Two Sections on camp construction. One Section working at MORY NORTH as above. A 3rd Section assisted in getting in material of 6th W.W.B. Pioneers.	WD
	14/4/17		2 Officers and 60 O.R. reported on infantry and Pack horse from Kew End of HORSE SHOE REDOUBT to SOUL ALLEY. One Officer and 24 O.R. on party to party of Pioneers of the 6th J.H. Bn being shifted — ensuring the economic of the draft from Pullbank to Camp ERVILLERS.	WD
	15/4/17		The Company moved into Camp at ERVILLERS.	WD
GOMIECOURT	16/4/17 17/4/17		Company sent out to erect Nissen Huts in D.A.C. Camp at before from Sections working on Nissen Camp MORY NORTH — NISSEN HUTS.	WD
	18/4/17 to 24/4/17		One section working on Nissen Camp MORY NORTH. One section on improving own camp. Two sections erecting NISSEN HUTS at DAC Camp GOMIECOURT and one section employed Roads at RESERVE BRIGADE Camp at B29 c2 7	WD

Army Form C. 2118.

WAR DIARY
INTELLIGENCE SUMMARY.
(Erase heading not required.)

DECEMBER 1917
SHEET NO 3.

Place	Date	Hour	Summary of Events and Information	Remarks and references to Appendices
2	23/12/17		Please see leave returned to the line in the PERCIVAL SECTOR. The enemy was nothing but on camp at ERICOURT.	
	24/12/17 and 25/12/17		The week was engaged in preparing puts for small rifle shells in front line and 029.d.4.9. The work on our own defences in DANBURY TRENCHES and RAILWAY RESERVE proceeded apace. Preparations were also made for shelter in support trench slums, LONDON SUPPORT and TOWER TRENCH. The billets improving lots at RENCHING BRIGADE CAMP B.28.c.2.7.	
	26/12/17		The action of the matter's Knife work was flowing from our position in front of [?] was in order the INTERMEDIATE LINE. The work was proceeding for shelters in rear [?] there was no rifle. One working party was used for shelter building in support and B.28.c.27 in [?].	
	27/12/17		Two working parties of PUDSEY SUPPORT TRENCH fatigues made on and were set also 25' of trench and 6 dugouts at PUDSEY SUPPORT, dug up and to end chatting reshaped on. The position making the two companies now actually holding the line up with R.282c.27 in reserve. The enemy completely sheltered on PUDSEY SUPPORT and [?] were in front line and TOWER TRENCH with [?]. [?]	

Army Form C. 2118.

WAR DIARY
or
INTELLIGENCE SUMMARY.
(Erase heading not required.)

437th (CHESHIRE) FIELD COMPANY, R.E.

DECEMBER 1917
SHEET N° 4.

Place	Date	Hour	Summary of Events and Information	Remarks and references to Appendices
	29/12/17		Reconnaissance was made of enemy wire supporting SOMERS and forty of TOWER TRENCH and found bad. If the majority of the wire is to be cut down in one day it is necessary and it opens to TOWER TRENCH and trenches to the N. side is shelter. In TOWER TRENCH and Somers trenches. The 3 sections working on the line to the 224th Field Coy R.E. and Junction to form the O.H. System and their Junction of Divisional RESERVE BRIGADE COMMANDER. R.28.c.2. which were ordered to this camp from KEMMEL on the date.	JM.
	30/12/17		Check parade and inspection of the Company.	JM
	31/12/17		Three sections continuing on wire cutting of this new camp. One section on [...] the [...] the huts to [...] the men to the [...] the [...] has been so unfit as on arrival [...] the shelter and [...] can hardly find quarters for both the men	JM

CASUALTIES

3/12/17. Capt. J. McGill posted to ROUEN to act as Instructor.
2/12/17 II Lt. C.H. ELCOCK joined the Company from 23rd Field Reserve.
10/12/17. N° 446875 Actg Cpl. H. SPARROCK Wounded H.M. M.T. on act.

[signature]
O.C. 437th (Cheshire) Field Coy RE.

3rd Division
War Diaries
498th Cheshire Field Coy.
~~January 1 to December 31~~

1918 JAN — 1919 OCT.

Army Form C. 2118.

JANUARY 1918. SHEET No 1.

WAR DIARY or INTELLIGENCE SUMMARY

(Erase heading not required.)

Place	Date	Hour	Summary of Events and Information	Remarks and references to Appendices
			438th (CHESHIRE) FIELD COY. R.E.	
	1/1/18 to 8/1/18		The Company were working on Huffled Group at MORY, whose shelters were mined out close chalk and boarding of same. The Company were also employed on improving their quarters and erecting stables and harness huts for the Mounted Section.	JW
	10/1/18		Three sections and Head Quarters moved to advanced billets in ST LEGER. Officers and N.C.O's were employed in reconnoitering work to be done in BATTLE ZONE between PELICAN AVENUE and the VENGER RIVER and at CROISILLES. The remaining section employed working on battle zone near MORY.	JW
	11/1/18		Three sections employed with 600 Infantry wiring and digging trench between PELICAN AVENUE and the VENGER RIVER. Traffic between MORY and SZ LEGER and 2200 men employed on road and possible repairs. Fourth section as before working NORTH of the VENGER RIVER.	JW
	12/1/18 to 18/1/18		The Sections employed with 100 Infantry up to 17/1/18 when employment then was increased to 600 Infantry. 4th section employed on new outposts trench...	JW
	19/1/18 to 21/1/18		Four sections on battle zone trench, wiring and their sections employed on outpost line dugouts by 600 Infantry. Trench communications from Pen 2.3 enhancing any digging on T 16 C 66. BULLECOURT. Trench map. 4th section employed as before.	JW
	22/1/18			JW
	24/1/18			JW

Army Form C. 2118.

WAR DIARY
INTELLIGENCE SUMMARY
(Erase heading not required.)

438TH (CHESHIRE) FIELD COMPANY, R.E.

JANUARY 1918 SHEET No. 2

Instructions regarding War Diaries and Intelligence Summaries are contained in F. S. Regs., Part II. and the Staff Manual respectively. Title pages will be prepared in manuscript.

Place	Date	Hour	Summary of Events and Information	Remarks and references to Appendices
	25/1/18		Two sections employed on infantry dugout on the ZOUAVE Wood system. Company on front of two lines with 100 Infantry to each. At MORY. Enemy kept very quiet.	AM.
	26/1/18		Three sections employed with 100 Infantry in wiring three sectors of the system at MORY to hinder an enemy infantry advance. Three sections at MORY, St LEGER sector, being such that the enemy at MORY was unable to carry out 207th Field Company RE at BOIRY BECQUERELLE T.1.C. method as an advanced party.	AM.
	27/1/18		The Company moved to BOIRY BECQUERELLE by route march and relieved the 207th Field Company RE. Headquarters and one section of Sappers to camp at T.1.c. Central. Three sections quartered to present Billets in HAC T TRENCH dugout No. 80. Provisional Rations remaining in Billets at T.7. Central.	AM.
	29/1/18		Three sections employed on improvement of the following trenches VIMY TRENCH, HUMP HOPE and FACTORY AVENUE. One section on improving the camp and putting huts from from tramway to kitchens.	AM.

WAR DIARY
INTELLIGENCE SUMMARY
(Erase heading not required.)

Army Form C. 2118.

438TH (CHESHIRE) FIELD COMPANY, R.E.

JANUARY 1918 / Sheet No. 3

Instructions regarding War Diaries and Intelligence Summaries are contained in F.S. Regs., Part II. and the Staff Manual respectively. Title pages will be prepared in manuscript.

Place	Date	Hour	Summary of Events and Information	Remarks and references to Appendices
	30/1/18		Wire entanglements on the following were kept up: JUNO TRENCH. HUMP LANE and FACTORY AVENUE. Improvement of parapet of SENSEE RESERVE TRENCH and to the TUNNEL TRENCH and CLAW TRENCH carried on as on the 29/1/18.	M
	31/1/18		Wire entanglements kept up of TUNNEL TRENCH and CLAW TRENCH and improvement of parapet of SENSEE RESERVE TRENCH carried on as before.	M
			CASUALTIES	
			Major J. P. WARD. Invalided M.C. NEW YEARS LIST 1918.	M
			C.S.M. T. R. Quigley. "Belgian Order Couronne" 3rd Journal Militaire No. 20.	M
			29/1/18 2 O.R. wounded 30/1/18.	M
			29/1/18 2 O.R. wounded at WKS. (at duty).	

John Mount Logan
Major
O.C. 438th Cheshire Field Company R.E.
1/2/18

Army Form C. 2118.

WAR DIARY
~~INTELLIGENCE SUMMARY~~

(Erase heading not required.)

488TH (CHESHIRE) FIELD COMPANY, R.E.

FEBRUARY 1918   Vol 37 sheet No 1.

Place	Date	Hour	Summary of Events and Information	Remarks and references to Appendices
	1/2/18			
	2/2/18		Three Sections in forward billets in SHAFT AV. engaged with Infantry for two days in clearing out mud and water the following trenches JUNO LANE, HUMP LANE and TENNIS Trench also in the SENSEE VALLEY also in digging an advance from shaft up CLAN Trench to SHAFT AV and digging SENSEE RESERVE T. One section of No. 4 Section engaged in dugouts in BOYELLES. One section engaged in strafing barrier on [?]	M
	3/2/18		[illegible section continues]	M
	6/2/18		[illegible] to shafts for the [illegible] the [illegible] cutting of [illegible] portion and [illegible] from shafts on [illegible] run and mud dugouts and also repair of [illegible] in [illegible] at BOYELLES. SLEEPER SIDING. and repair of a top course to the SLEEPER BOYELLES ROAD	M
	7/2/18		Six Sections formed into Companies on repair and repair of the [illegible] through FIN LANE, FAG LANE and on lorries from also the Lorries [illegible] ROYAL DUMP. to MEWLAS AV. One section of men took on Sleeper repair the	M
	11/2/18		work at SLEEPER SIDING. and repair of sidings to entrances to dugouts ROAD.	

Army Form C. 2118.

WAR DIARY
INTELLIGENCE SUMMARY.
(Erase heading not required.)

483RD (CHESHIRE) FIELD COMPANY, R.E.

FEBRUARY 1917

Place	Date	Hour	Summary of Events and Information	Remarks and references to Appendices
	14/2/17 to 18/2/17		Men engaged in forward continued work on FRAY LANE, FUN LANE and TUNNEL TRENCH. Work generally work on Coy. O.P. & HINDENBURG LANE. Section of men holds employment work on protection of huts in Bivouac camp.	
	19/2/17 to 24/2/17		Men continued work on above. Men employed work on FUN LANE, TUNNEL TRENCH as before also in completing work on CORPS O.P. Reported back yesterday at JANET AVENUE reference 7 SHAFT 15] — TUNNEL T and 7 recommenced one evening work northerly 30 yds. Two sections of men before were employed in putting huts in the new camps at Y.M.C.A. and at the DIVISIONAL Head Quarters.	
	25/2/17 to 28/2/17		Men continued work on supplying work on the above. Number TUNNEL TRENCH, JUN LANE and FOR LANE. Preparing at can trench in protection that general party have attacked. Men continued work engaged in supplying and manning of JUNO LANE FOR LANE and reference of party of trench on to the of CLAW TRENCH and TUNNEL TRENCH.	

Army Form C. 2118.

WAR DIARY
INTELLIGENCE SUMMARY

(Erase heading not required.)

Instructions regarding War Diaries and Intelligence Summaries are contained in F. S. Regs., Part II. and the Staff Manual respectively. Title pages will be prepared in manuscript.

438th (CHESHIRE) FIELD COMPANY, R.E.

FEBRUARY 1918 Vol no 3

Place	Date	Hour	Summary of Events and Information	Remarks and references to Appendices
Cambrai	4th February 1918		10 R. Inspected	AM
"	5 "		" 10 R. "	AM

John Monad Frazer RE(T)
Major 438th Field Company R.E.

3rd Divisional Engineers

438th (Cheshire) FIELD COMPANY R. E.

MARCH 1918

War Diary

438th (Cheshire) Fd. Co. R.E.

Month of March 1918

WAR DIARY
INTELLIGENCE SUMMARY

Army Form C.2118.

488th (Cheshire) Field Company, R.E.

March 1918

Vol 38

Place	Date	Hour	Summary of Events and Information	Remarks and references to Appendices
	1/3/18		Headquarters and one section sent on Rifle Range at BOIRY-BECQUERELLE. One section working by day on the line on FOLANE Work on the explosive van handed over to the 207th Field Eng. R.E. Work now moved on expg.? R.F.A. H.Q. at FICHEUX	JM
	2/3/18		One section now working on work at FICHEUX tramway. One section now sound? from finished bullets at shafts 80 m. on the right bank.	JM / JM
	3/3/18		One section continued work as on the report. 3 sections bathed and divisional baths in thier over Line	JM
	4/3/18		2 sections have completed their laying of EGRET TRENCH & then section on replacement shoring of CROW TRENCH the sinking? ??? on these over posts and embarking track behind at SWINDON SIDING.	JM
	5/3/18 6/3/18		3 sections engaged on work on the line on EGRET TRENCH and on Hay GUNNERS RESERVE. One section est. cow H.Q. on abandoned ?? at DURHAM LINE, MERCATEL, and work for the shop at HENIN DEUP.	JM

Army Form C.2118.

WAR DIARY
or
INTELLIGENCE SUMMARY

(Erase heading not required.)

488TH (CHESHIRE) FIELD COMPANY, R.E.

No. 2

MARCH 1918

Place	Date	Hour	Summary of Events and Information	Remarks and references to Appendices
	7/3/18		Two sections employed in the line on the 1st. One section employed in tents in DURHAM LINES and at HEWIN DUMP. One section employed from reveille at N.21.c.1.d. & N.27.d.	
	8/3/18		One section forward to forward System of SEGARD & Enemy in DUBIANT Tench at N.22.a.56. N.21.S.I.E.SW. & Enemy relation employed on the hut in site and also commenced wiring POSTET AVENUE. One Enfilaved by gun employed in forming of new subterranean huts in DURHAM LINES and improving huts in DURHAM LINES.	
	9/3/18 10/3/18		Two sections continued work as for 8/3. SHARK AVENUE has now been completed. Work on S.M. P.M. & GR.	
	12/3		Task and work similar in the line & when Employed Subway. One section two employed bringing up 37,500 rounds for the COLORS RINGS between HENINEL and HANCOURT. One section on laying TANK MINES in H. GARNET POINTE. SUGAR RESERVE and BISON RESERVE.	
	13/3/18		Two sections in the line employed as on the 12th. Posts near Enfilave and Post Employment as before. West Section Wire revailed.	

Army Form C. 2118.

WAR DIARY
or
INTELLIGENCE SUMMARY.
(Erase heading not required.)

MARCH 1918

Place	Date	Hour	Summary of Events and Information	Remarks and references to Appendices
	27/3/18		Coys. officers were engaged in stopping and warning the	
	29/3/18		PURPLE LINE, met [illegible] Fitz Herbert and fell away of the Transport, and details moved to GROUVILLE	
			Coys. returned from Transport and all were at GROUVILLE and the whole Company prepared by route march to SOUX en ARTOIS.	
	29/3/18		The Company proceeded by road march to IVERGNY.	
			The Company arrived in billets at IVERGNY.	

Br [signature]

2. O. R. [illegible]

29/3/18 Lt. V. T. ROBERTSON left Batt. [illegible]

Lt. [illegible]

30/3/18 2nd Lt. S. LE STEELEY joined the Unit

[signatures]

3rd Divisional Engineers

WAR DIARY

438th (CHESHIRE) FIELD COMPANY R. E.

APRIL 1918

Army Form C. 2118.

438TH (CHESHIRE) FIELD COMPANY, R.E.

SHEET No 1
APRIL 1918

WAR DIARY / INTELLIGENCE SUMMARY.
(Erase heading not required.)

Instructions regarding War Diaries and Intelligence Summaries are contained in F.S. Regs., Part II. and the Staff Manual respectively. Title pages will be prepared in manuscript.

Place	Date	Hour	Summary of Events and Information	Remarks and references to Appendices
IVERGNY	1/4/18		Dismounted personnel proceeded by march to ROZIERE and by bus to AUCHEL. Mounted and transport by march IVERGNY to ROZIERE to AUCHEL.	
MAISNIL-ST POL	2/4/18		Dismounted personnel in billets AUCHEL. Mounted and transport by march route MAISNIL ST POL to AUCHEL	
	3/4/18		In billets AUCHEL	
	4/4/18		Coy proceeded by march route AUCHEL to FOUQUIERES	
	5/4/18		Coy FOUQUIERES - refitting	
	6/4/18		" Resting and Church parade	
	7/4/18		" Church parade	
	8/4/18 — 10/4/18		" Training	
	11/4/18		Proceeded by route march to VENDIN LES BETHUNE — 8th Inf Bde Concentration Area. Nos 1 & 2 sections proceeded to work in line at 10.30pm. No 1 & 2 " " to prepare bridges for demolition on the BASSEE Canal. Company assembled and proceeded to hold Part of line with 8th KORL Regt.	
	12/4/18		Returned to Canal Bank and billeted in barges. Transport moved to near CHOQUES.	
	13/4/18		Supplying a carrying party and preparing barges and bridges for demolition. No 3 section returns to ferrying limbers	

Army Form C. 2118.

438TH (CHESHIRE) FIELD COMPANY, R.E.

WAR DIARY
or
INTELLIGENCE SUMMARY
(Erase heading not required)

Sheet No 2
APRIL 1918

Place	Date	Hour	Summary of Events and Information	Remarks and references to Appendices
	14/4/18		No 3 section proceeded forward. Company continued work as for 13/4/18	JHCG
	15/4/18		Company returned to Neuogod lines. 2 sections at Dam, 2 sections at 5.30am No 1 section proceeded to work on reserve line. Remainder of Coy moved by road route to FOUQUEREUIL	JHCG
	16/4/18		At FOUQUEREUIL. No 1,2,3,4 sections working on GHQ 14 Bde Sector	JHCG
	17/4/18		No 1 Section ditto " " Canal La Bassée	JHCG
	18/4/18		No 2TH " foot bridge	JHCG
			No 3 Sector & point No 2 pontoon bridge on La Bassée Canal	JHCG
			No 2TH " foot bridge	
			No 1 " barge "	
			No 14H " "	
	19/4/18		No 14H section demolition of bridges & culverts	JHCG
	20/4/18		No 3 section demolition of bridges and routes bridge guard	JHCG
	21/4/18		No 2 " " wiring Liverpool line	JHCG
	22/4/18		No 1TH section " " Liverpool line	JHCG
	23/4/18		No 2+4 " " Wiring Liverpool line	JHCG
	24/4/18		No 1 + 2 " No 3 Bridge guards	JHCG
	25/4/18		Work in forward area & bridge guard. Ditto Guard relieved over to 465 Fd.C.R.E. (4th Div)	JHCG
	26/4/18		No 1+2 sections marking route near Annezin Re Dump. No 4 " " Company out reserve line near HINGES	JHCG

Army Form C. 2118.

438TH (CHESHIRE) FIELD COMPANY. R.E.
SHEET No 3
APRIL 1918

WAR DIARY

INTELLIGENCE SUMMARY.
(Erase heading not required.)

Instructions regarding War Diaries and Intelligence Summaries are contained in F.S. Regs., Part II. and the Staff Manual respectively. Title pages will be prepared in manuscript.

Place	Date	Hour	Summary of Events and Information	Remarks and references to Appendices
At Fouquereuil	27/4/18		No 2 & 4 sections supervising digging of reserve line near Hinges No 1 & 3 " working at Annezin Dump	JWC
	28/4/18		" " Work Co fer 27th. Moved camp to Revillon Wood near Choques	JWC
At Revellion Wood	29/4/18		No 3 section on Fickes Bridge over stream between Laures and Bassee Canals No 2 & 4 sections on reserve line near Hinges	JWC
	30/4/18		" " Taking over work from 56th Field Co R.E. No 2 section and part of No 1. proceeded to take over bridge guards.	JWC

Casualties — 8 o.r. wounded

✗

✗ (2 of above strained or hurt)

John Chark ---- Major R.E.

O.C. 438th (Ches) Field Co R.E.
1/5/18

438 Field Coy.
2nd Pl.
1. Pl. Sgt.
2. ...

1. Tonight the 438/75 Grids will blow up all
   Stuffers bridges & culverts over the Stream line, & replace
   them with planks or duckboards bridges.
2. Craters will be blown in the following places
   Xroads in X.21.A. & road junction W.15.c.5.9.
   road junction X.21.B.35.
3. 438 Pr. officer in will report to Coy in touch with Bn.
   in whose area the demolitions are being carried out.

M.613

Bm

Army Form C. 2118.

SHEET 1.

438TH (CHESHIRE) FIELD COMPANY, R.E.

WAR DIARY
or
INTELLIGENCE SUMMARY.
(Erase heading not required.)

MAY 1918

Place	Date	Hour	Summary of Events and Information	Remarks and references to Appendices
Forward billets YENDIN	1-8		Work in Right Sub sector, with 8th Inf. Bde. Hacketts furnished guards for Bridges on LAWE and LA BASSEE Canals. 2½ sections on Battn HQ in camps, Brunk - La Bassee Canal, and improving line of front+support line. Co relieved on night 8/9 by 529th Fd Coy and returned to rear billets	H.G.
Rear billets REVEILLON WOOD	9-12		In reserve. Preparing Bridges for demolition on Clarence River, and forward billets for CHOQUES	H.G.
Rear billets REVEILLON WOOD			Relieved 564 Field Coy in Left Sub Sector on night 12/13.	H.G.
"	13-20		1 Section furnished guards for Bridges La BASSEE Canal + maintained Bridges. Brunk charges, and kept canal boats clear.	H.G.
"	13		1 Section on Battn HQ near HINGES W.15.c.1.9. 2 Section on forward billets near CUCUQUES	H.G.
"	14		" 1 Section on forward billets. 1 Section on pit prop	H.G.
"	15		" Bridge BETHUNE relay	H.G.
"	16		" " ditto	H.G.
"			W.15637 " 1 section towing two logs out bridge up canal	H.G.
"	17		" 1 section building cork bridge at R.E. Dump	H.G.
"	18		" " taking up and launching bridge	H.G.

WAR DIARY or INTELLIGENCE SUMMARY

Army Form C. 2118.

438TH (CHESHIRE) FIELD COMPANY, R.E.

MAY 1918

SHEET 2

Place	Date	Hour	Summary of Events and Information	Remarks and references to Appendices
REVEILLON WOOD	19		1 section Bdg't HQ near HINGES W15d 37. 1 section on floating Bridges La BASSÉE Canal	JHG
	20		1 " " and COY W15 a 47. 1 section on Emergency Bridge at LONDON BRIDGE	JHG
	21		Relieved by 529th Fld Co. RE.	JHG
	22		1 section on Baths at CHOQUES. Two sections working in Camp.	JHG
			ditto. 1 section on emergency bridge + ramp LONDON BR. 1 section on concrete MGE near LE JAUDRY Farm W22 a 7·9	JHG
	23		ditto ditto and casting materials for MGE emp.	JHG
	24		1 section on Baths at CHOQUES. 1 section on Emergency Bridge LONDON BR. Two sections concrete MG Emp. near LE JAUDRY FARM	JHG
	25		2 sections MG emp. near LE JAUDRY Farm. Emergency Bridge near LONDON BR. W22 a 7·9	JHG
	26		do	JHG
	27		do Preparing bridge for demolition	JHG
	28		do Preparing bridge at E5 a 25. Weeran Dudo1 Emergency Bridge. Baths at CHOQUES	JHG
	29		do Preparing for demolition Bridge at E10 a 98	JHG
	30		1 section in Camp on material for MGE emp.	JHG
			Relieved 56th Field Co. R.E. in Rgts (HINGES) Sub section ½ section proceeded to furnish guards for Bridges etc.	JHG

Army Form C. 2118.

MAY 1918

400th (CHESHIRE) FIELD COMPANY, R.E.

SHEET 3

WAR DIARY
INTELLIGENCE SUMMARY

(Erase heading not required.)

Place	Date	Hour	Summary of Events and Information	Remarks and references to Appendices
	31.		1 section on M.G. Emp M.22.a.7-9 near LE JANDREY FARM. 1/2 section on 40 B.o.	J.O.G.
			RFA Headquarters in BETHUNE. 1/2 sections on bridge guard on	
			LA BASSEE and LAWE Canals.	
			Casualties for month	
			1LW C.H. ELCOCK wounded 1-5-18	
			" Lieut J.J. FISHER wounded (gas) 26-5-18 31/5/18	J.O.G.
			Killed 1 - O.R.	
			wounded shell fire 4 - O.R. including 31/5/18 remaining at duty	
			" gas 26 - O.R. " 12 "	
			1LW A.P. WEIR joined unit 9-5-18	
			1LW T.M. COTTRELL " 29-5-18	
			C/M Corps LEWIS awarded D.C.M. for gallantry in the field 4-5-18	
			Auth XIII Corps 1647a 19-5-18	

John O'Farrell Prager, Lt RE
O.C. No 3 Sth Cheshire Field Coy RE
1/6/18.

Army Form C. 2118.

SHEET No 1

438TH (CHESHIRE)
FLD Co ?????
June 19/18
Vol 41

WAR DIARY
of
INTELLIGENCE SUMMARY.
(Erase heading not required.)

Instructions regarding War Diaries and Intelligence Summaries are contained in F. S. Regs., Part II. and the Staff Manual respectively. Title pages will be prepared in manuscript.

Place	Date	Hour	Summary of Events and Information	Remarks and references to Appendices
BOIS DE PREVILLON	1/6/18 – 30/6/18		Location. Bridge Guards, demolition parties La Bassée and La Lawe Canals. Repairing Bridges. Testing and repairing charges.	ShSh
Work in	1/6/18 – 30/6/18		1 section on concrete MG emplacements near LE JAVARIE FARM	ShSh
LOCON SECTOR	22/6/18 – 30/6/18		" " Boston N.G" on CAMEL LANE near LAWE CANAL	ShSh
	1/6/18		Enlarging and improving 8th Inf Bde HQ & 42 Bde RFA HQ near BETHUNE	ShSh
	2/6/18		do do	ShSh
	3/6/18		do do	ShSh
	4/6/18 – 6/6/18		Co. for 2/6/18. Footbridges in ABERDEEN LINE. Explant shelter for G.H.Q. ABERDEEN LINE	ShSh
	7/6/18		Co. for 2/6/18	ShSh
	8/6/18	-	Do Improving HQ 42 Bde RFA and started work on 8th Inf Bde HQ in	ShSh
	9/6/18		HQ 42 Bde RFA and 8th Inf Bde HQ - Canal Bank	ShSh
	10/6/18 – 13/6/18		8th Inf Bde HQ and Brewery BETHUNE. Strengthening & improving Bridges on LA BASSEE CANAL for DA.	ShSh
	14/6/18		Co. for 10/6/18 - Clearing Crossing of bridges on LA BASSEE Canal Bridge on Chalico Rue for DA.	ShSh
	15/6/18		Co. for 10/6/18	ShSh
	16/6/18		Co. for 10/6/18	ShSh
	17/6/18		Co. for 10/6/18	ShSh
	18/6/18		Co. for 10/6/18 Work at BREWERY completed	ShSh

(A7092). Wt. W12859/M1293. 750,000. 1/17. D. D. & L., Ltd. Forms/C2118/4.

Army Form C. 2118.

Sheet No 2

June 1918

WAR DIARY
INTELLIGENCE SUMMARY.
(Erase heading not required)

438TH (CHESHIRE) FIELD COMPANY, R.E.

Instructions regarding War Diaries and Intelligence Summaries are contained in F. S. Regs., Part II. and the Staff Manual respectively. Title pages will be prepared in manuscript.

Place	Date	Hour	Summary of Events and Information	Remarks and references to Appendices
HQ at Bois de Reveillon	19/6/18		Improving and enlarging 8th Inf Bde HQ on Canal Bank W 29c 5-6 Building MG Dug outs near Woodyard Bethune	JH.G
Work in Locon Sector	20/6/18		Ao for 19/6/18 and removing metre gauge railway track over ABERDEEN LINE W 29c 5-7	JH.G
	21/6/18		Ao for 20/6/18 and improving cellar for Staff Captain 8th/Bde W 29c 1-3	JH.G
	22/6/18		Ao for 19/6/18	JH.G
	23/6/18		Ao for 19/6/18 and over hauling charges on bridges in W 28 and W 29	JH.G
	24/6/18		Ao for 19/6/18, over hauling charges on bridges in E Sa. Elephant shelter for Co H.Q. at W 18c 9-8 unloading material for bridge at W 29 c 9-1	JH.G
	25/6/18		Ao for 24/6/18 unloading material for Locon Road Bridge at W 29c 9-1	JH.G
	26/6/18		Ao for 25/6/18 over hauling bridges in E rod	JH.G
	27/6/18		Ao for 24/6/18 ex-cav¹ over hauling bridges. Erecting steel work bridge W 29c 9-1 JH.G and boring camp	JH.G
	28/6/18		Ao for 27/6/18	JH.G
	29/6/18		Ao for 28/6/18 Locon Road Bridge completed W 29c 9-1	JH.G
	30/6/18		Batt. HQ on Canal Lane Concreting walls. No 2 section relieved No 3 on demolition parties and bridge guards for LA BASSEE and LA LAWE Canals	JH.G
			MG Dug Outs W 29c 5-7 Top filling on elephant shelter 8th Inf Bde HQ W 29c 5-6 Elephant shelter for Inwell office fixing elephant shelters.	JH.G

CASUALTIES

1 O.R. wounded 30/6/18 to attached Coy wounded (Accidentally) (Accidentally) (sleeping forward)

J.H.G.G Capt E

J.H.G.G (Geo) Field C.R.E

o/c 438th (Che) Field Coy RE

Army Form C. 2118.

WAR DIARY
or
INTELLIGENCE SUMMARY.
(Erase heading not required.)

438TH (CHESHIRE) FIELD COMPANY, R.E.

JULY 1918. Vol 4

Place	Date	Hour	Summary of Events and Information	Remarks and references to Appendices
H.Q at BOIS DE REVEILLON	1/7/18 – 31/7/18		1 Section Bridge Guards and demolition parties LA BASSEE and LA LAWE Canals. Repairing Bridges. Testing and repairing charges. Entrenching contdt.	A.J.S.G.
took in	1/7/18		troops on LA LAWE Canal.	A.J.S.G.
LOCON SECTOR	– 27/7/18		1 Section on Concrete Batty. H.Q. on CANAL LAWE near LAWE CANAL.	A.J.S.G.
	28/7/18 – 31/7/18		1 Section on Concrete Shelter at W.18.C.21. Dump Point.	A.J.S.G.
	2/7/18 – 20/7/18		Blazic Concrete Shelter at W.18.C.2.1.	A.J.S.G.
	1/7/18		Enlarging and improving 8" Inf. Bde. HQ near BETHUNE	A.J.S.G.
	2/7/18 ao 1st 1/7/18			A.J.S.G.
	ao 1st 4/7/18		Constructing shelters dr Eng. H.Q.=M G. Dugout	A.J.S.G.
	ao 1st 1/7/18			A.J.S.G.
	4/7/18 – 8/7/18		New H.Q. for 42nd Bde. R.F.A. adjacent to Inf. Bde. HQ	A.J.S.G.
	9/7/18		Constructing shelters for Eng. H.Q.	A.J.S.G.
	10/7/18 ao 1st 9/7/18			A.J.S.G.
	11/7/18 ao 1st 9/7/18			A.J.S.G.
	12/7/18 ao 1st 9/7/18			A.J.S.G.
	13/7/18 ao 1st 12/7/18		and increased accommodation at 2nd Inf. Bde. HQ and M.G. Shelter	A.J.S.G.
	13/7/18 – 17/7/18 18/7/18 – 31/7/18		ao 1st 12/7/18 and actions network from heavy bridge at W.24.C.9.1. and subterraneous entracts, improvements in PERTH LINE	A.J.S.G.

Army Form C. 2118.

438TH (CHESHIRE) FIELD COMPANY R.E.

SHEET N° 2

WAR DIARY
INTELLIGENCE SUMMARY
(Erase heading not required.)

Place	Date	Hour	Summary of Events and Information	Remarks and references to Appendices
H.Q. AT BOIS DE REVEILLON	23/7/18		O.o. for 22/7/18 and instructing R.A.P. at W.23.b.85.15	H.725.
	24/7/18	K.25/7/8	O.o. for 23/7/18 and instructing dolin for O.P. at W.18.d.46 and O.P. in chimney at W.18.d.82	H.726.
Work in LOCON SECTOR	25/7/18		O.o. for 24/7/18 and instructing Rat Buller for Patrols at W.23.b.75.15	H.727.
	26/7/18		O.o. for 26/7/18. Chimney O.P. completed. No.3 sectn. started No.2.m demolition	H.728.
	28/7/18 to 29/7/18 3/7/18		O.o. for 26/7/18. R.A.P at W.23.b.85.15; O.P at W.18.d.46; Patrol Rat Buller; M.G. Cn. Shelters and intervening infantry or improvements to PERTH LINE	H.729.
			CASUALTIES	
	7/7/18		A/Captain J. McGILL left to take command of 7th 3rd Cn. R.E	
			Lieut. H.J.F. GOURLEY rejoined Cn. fm C.R.E.	

John Blandfryse R.E??
O.C 438th London Field Coy R.E
1/8/18

WAR DIARY
INTELLIGENCE SUMMARY

Army Form C. 2118.

433rd (CHESHIRE) ? ? ?Y. R.E.

AUGUST 1918. Sheet No 1.

VC 43

(Erase heading not required.)

Place	Date	Hour	Summary of Events and Information	Remarks and references to Appendices
H.Q. at BOIS DE REVEILLON	1-8-18 to 7-8-18		1 Section. Bridge Guards and demolition parties LA BASSÉE and LA LAWE Canals. Repairing Bridges; testing and repairing charges	H.Y.S.
Work in Locon Sector	1-8-18 to 7-8-18		1 Section on Curaulo Shelter at W.18.c.21. Strong Point	H.Y.S.
	1-8-18		R.A.P. at W.23.G.8.15: bank material completed; Shelter for M.G. Cry.	
	7-8-18		O.P. Shelter at W.18.d.4.6 completed; Improvements at B.H. Out Post. HQ in canal bank BETHUNE completed; Deterior? defences? on Improvements at PERTH LINE bank	H.Y.S.
			All work handed over to 81st Cny. R.E. on relief.	
	7-8-18		Dismounted personnel proceed by bus to MAREST & LE BOUDOU CHOCQUES. Mounted and transport by march to MAREST.	H.Y.S.
	8-8-18		At MAREST – refitting and resting.	H.Y.S.
	9-8-18 to 12-8-18		" "	H.Y.S.
	13-8-18		Dismounted personnel to BRYAS by motor lorry, thence by train to WARLIN COURT HALTE & by route march to WARLUZEL	H.Y.S.
	13/14-8-18		Mounted and Transport by route march, night only march, to WAVRANS	H.Y.S.

Army Form C. 2118.

438TH (CHESHIRE) FIELD COMPANY. R.E.

AUGUST 1918
SHEET No. 2

WAR DIARY
INTELLIGENCE SUMMARY.
(Erase heading not required.)

Instructions regarding War Diaries and Intelligence Summaries are contained in F. S. Regs., Part II and the Staff Manual respectively. Title pages will be prepared in manuscript.

Place	Date	Hour	Summary of Events and Information	Remarks and references to Appendices
	14/15.8.18		Mounted and Transport by night road WAVRANS to WARLUZEL.	H.J.S.
	14.8.18		at WARLUZEL. Dismounted trainers dumps afternoon.	H.J.S.
	15.8.18 to 19.8.18		" Training of mounted and dismounted.	
	19/20.8.18		Whole Company, incl Transport by route march from WARLUZEL to MONCHY-AU-BOIS — Dismounted proceeded and to POMMIER — mounted transport and details	H.J.S.
	20.8.18		No 3 Section and details. 1 Officer & 4 O.R. Reconnaissance with 8th Brigade in readiness for operations commencing 21.8.18.	H.J.S.
	21.8.18		Dismounted proceeded with 2nd Royal Scots from MONCHY-AU-BOIS to PURPLE LINE Trench between MONCHY and ADINFER WOOD.	H.J.S.
	22.8.18		3. Section employed on making AYETTE-COURCELLES Road. 1 Officer & 4 O.R. rejoined Coy from Brigade.	H.J.S.
	23.8.18		3. Section moved forward to "MOYBLAIN TRENCH" in rear of COURCELLES-LE-COMTE	H.J.S.
	24.8.18		3 Section employed on COURCELLES - ERVILLERS Road. These sections moved back. Transport and details moved from POMMIER to camp in front of ADINFER WOOD.	H.J.S.
	25.8.18 26.8.18 27.8.18		No 3 Section rejoined Coy: Company resting and refitting.	H.J.S.
	28.8.18		4. Section worked on AYETTE - MOYENVILLE Road. No. 2 Section attached to 8th Inf. Brigade for work AYETTE-MOYENVILLE Road with Infantry.	H.J.S.
			3 Section, H.Q and Transport proceeded by route march ADINFER WOOD to MOYENNEVILLE.	H.J.S.

Army Form C. 2118.

WAR DIARY
or
INTELLIGENCE SUMMARY.
(Erase heading not required.)

435th (CHESHIRE) FIELD COMPANY. R.E.

AUGUST 1918 SHEET No. 3.

Instructions regarding War Diaries and Intelligence Summaries are contained in F. S. Regs., Part II. and the Staff Manual respectively. Title pages will be prepared in manuscript.

Place	Date	Hour	Summary of Events and Information	Remarks and references to Appendices
	29.8.18		3 Sections unit transport moved on road unfortunately to/from HAMELINCOURT – MAISON ROUGE FARM ROAD.	M.708.
	30.8.18		3 " " " " " " " " " MAISON ROUGE FARM –	M.734.
	31.8.18		Whole Company less No 2 Section transport standing by for orders. ST LEGER ROAD	M.735.
			CASUALTIES	
	27.8.18		Major J.R. GREIG (attached for instruction from 30.5.18) left to report to Director of Works — Fifth Army	M.708.
	9.8.18		Lt. R. McCREA joined from Base	

John Edward, Major R.E.(T)
O.C. 435. (Ches). Field Coy. R.E.
1.9.18.

Army Form C. 2118.

WAR DIARY
INTELLIGENCE SUMMARY
(Erase heading not required.)

Army CHEESHIRE **FIELD COMPANY, R.E.** 3rd Div

Month and Year: SEPTEMBER 1918
Commanding Officer: [illegible]
SHEET No. 1.

Instructions regarding War Diaries and Intelligence Summaries are contained in F.S. Regs., Part II. and the Staff Manual respectively. Title pages will be prepared in manuscript.

Place	Date	Hour	Summary of Events and Information	Remarks and references to Appendices
	1/9/18 – 30/9/18		No. 2 Section (Inf.) attached to 8th Inf. Bde. for work and transport	H.J.K.
	1.9.18		3 Sections worked during day improving & repairing road JUDAS FARM to ST LEGER	H.J.K.
	2.9.18		H.Q., 3 Sections and transport moved to SENSEE Valley, South of ST LEGER in evening	H.J.K.
			H.Q., 3 Sections and transport moved to North of ST LEGER	H.J.K.
			2 Sections with limbers worked on improvement of L'HOMME MORT – ECOUST Road by day	H.J.K.
	3.9.18		" " ST LEGER – ECOUST Road by night	H.J.K.
			4 Q., 3 Sections and transport moved to area South of MOYENNEVILLE	H.J.K.
			No. 2 Section rejoined Company at MOYENNEVILLE	
	4.9.18		Whole Company with transport moved to area between L'HOMME MORT and ST LEGER	H.J.K.
			3 Sections worked with transport on improvement of VRAUCOURT SUCRERIE – ECOUST Road by day	H.J.K.
			1 Section in reserve worked on Camp improvements	
	5.9.18		4 Sections worked with transport on improvement of VRAUCOURT SUCRERIE – ECOUST Road by day	H.J.K.
			Transport sent to WARLENCOURT to pick up Pontoons & Superstructure dumped on 19.8.18	
	6.9.18		Whole Company with transport moved to area N.J. HUMBERCAMP	H.J.K.
	7.9.18		Transport & Company returned with Pontoons & Superstructure to HUMBERCAMP	H.J.K.
			Officers and Division N.C.O's to ROSEL by lorry to inspect R.B. Span bridge under construction	
	8.9.18		Company refitting and bathing	H.J.K.
			1 Officer and T.O.R. to BOYELLES to cut bridging material all day	
			Church Parade.	
	9.9.18		1 Officer and T.O.R. to ROSEL to inspect bridge under construction at ROSEL and to assist in work	H.J.K.
			1. Bathing Parties to [illegible] Baths	H.J.K.
			2. Lecture by O.C. B.D. & [illegible]	H.J.K.
			3 agreed on Lewis Gunnery	

WAR DIARY of INTELLIGENCE SUMMARY

Army Form C. 2118.

438TH (CHESHIRE) FIELD COMPANY R.E.

SEPTEMBER 1918

SHEET No. 2.

Place	Date	Hour	Summary of Events and Information	Remarks and references to Appendices
	10.9.18		1 Officer and 7 O.R. to ROSEL to inspect and assist in constructing 120 Span bridge.	M/KR
	11.9.18		2 Sections Pontoon bridge practice	M/RS
	12.9.18		Whole Company practice	M/RS
	13.9.18		Whole company with transport moved to area South of AYETTE North of VRAUCOURT	M/RS
	14.9.15		do	M/RS
	15.9.18		Company resting - clean arms, clothing and kit inspections.	
	16.9.18		to the Recovery Various Spare and other sides. Parameter.	JM
			Company moved to BEAUMETZ two transport park at junction to MORCHIES-ETUM	JM
	17.9.18		1 Section proceeded to HERMIES.	
			Recce Beaumetz working on Sunken road on N.C 20.C BEAUMETZ. 1 Section returned to Transport lines. 1 Party on Reconnaissance of the Canal DUNORD. 1 party working on Billets at BEAUMETZ	JM
	18/9/18		1 Section on road as above. 1 Section in advance Billet Head Quarters HERMIES. 1 Section on builders and coverings of Canal du NORD Bridge tackled as above.	JM
	19/9/18 20/9/18		Company employed as above and one party on Temporary Bridges at BEAUMETZ	JM

BEAUMETZ

Army Form C. 2118.

435TH (CHESHIRE) FIELD COMPANY, R.E.

WAR DIARY
INTELLIGENCE SUMMARY

SEPTEMBER 1918
SHEET No 3

(Erase heading not required.)

Instructions regarding War Diaries and Intelligence Summaries are contained in F.S. Regs., Part II. and the Staff Manual respectively. Title pages will be prepared in manuscript.

Place	Date	Hour	Summary of Events and Information	Remarks and references to Appendices
	20/9/18		Company employed as on the 19th and were employed on 3rd Divisional advanced H.Q. and remained as 62nd Divisional H.Q.	
	21/9/18		As above.	
	22/9/18		As above. No 2 Section relieved No 4 Section the Light parties on Transport lines on 23/9/18.	
	23/9/18			
	24/9/18		Company engaged as above and party on work on the Bridge by-pass north of Pont Fixe BEAUMETZ completed.	
	25/9/18			
	26/9/18		Company employed as above and Bidding of the trees. Dismounted Section of company moved to HERMIES.	
	27/9/18		1 officer and 50 O.Rs. were employed on reconnaissance 3 Sections on Slab road K 26 c & d. Company appear not now HERMIES	
	28/9/18		Company employed on Slab road as above.	
	29/9/18		Company employed as above.	
	30/9/18		Company moved to HAVRINCOURT AREA K 22 c & 25	

Gunwalloe
A.F.

Major R.E.
O/C 435th (Cheshire) F.Co. R.E.
1/10/18

Army Form C. 2118.

438TH (CHESHIRE) FIELD COMPANY, R.E.

OCTOBER 1918
SHEET No 1.

WAR DIARY
INTELLIGENCE SUMMARY.
(Erase heading not required.)

Place	Date	Hour	Summary of Events and Information	Remarks and references to Appendices
	1.10.18		Company and Transport moved to FLESQUIERES One officer + party with half Coy: cart proceeded for reconnaissance to MARCOING	2/4/78
	4.10.18 to 5.10.18		One officer + small party proceeded on reconnaissance for locating foot bridge MARCOING	2/4/78
	5.10.18		2 Sections of Sappers employed with transport in 2 reliefs laying of horse water- ing ponds on L'ESCAUT River and CANAL DE L'ESCAUT at MARCOING	4/78
	6.10.18		1 officer and half section Sappers repairing foot bridge over CANAL DE L'ESCAUT at MARCOING	4/78
			1 officer and one section completing work on horse watering ponds on L'ESCAUT River and CANAL DE L'ESCAUT at MARCOING	3/4/78
	7.10.18		4 Sections Physical training in Camp. Clean arms and kit inspection	4/78
	8.10.18		2 Sections with transport making horse watering ponds east of CANAL DE L'ESCAUT near MARCOING	4/78
	9.10.18		2 Sections Bayonet training and Camp improvements	4/78
			Do on 8.10.18	4/78
	10.10.18		2 Sections with transport in 2 reliefs repairing lock arch bridge at L.22.b.1.1. in MARCOING	4/78
	10.10.18		2 Sections training and Camp improvements	4/78
			Do on 10.10.18	
	11.10.18		2 Sections with transport in 2 reliefs repairing lock arch bridge at L.22.G.1.1. in MARCOING	4/78
			1 section with transport moved to forward billets in MARCOING. Employed on repairing water bridge and bridge and maintaining dam also in running and erecting bridge from MARCOING at CREVECOEUR	4/78
			1 Section in Camp improvements	4/78

Army Form C. 2118.

438TH
(CHESHIRE)
FIELD COMPANY. R.E.

OCTOBER 1918
SHEET No. 2

WAR DIARY
INTELLIGENCE SUMMARY.
(Erase heading not required.)

Place	Date	Hour	Summary of Events and Information	Remarks and references to Appendices
	13.10.18		1 section working on 2nd Div. H.Q. in PLESQUIERES patrolling both banks and bridge in Marcoing area; also in erecting bumping jetty in ~ CREVECOEUR	H.J.R.
	14.10.18		remaining bank and bridge L.22.G.11. in MARCOING. Physical exercise and Recruiting Games	H.J.R.
			As per Div. H.Q. in PLESQUIERES; 1½ section Training in Camp	H.J.R.
	15.10.18		1 " " with transport repairs bridge at L.23.G.08; ½ section with transport repairs to bridge at L.22.6.11 in CREVECOEUR	H.J.R.
			1 " " patrolling both banks and bridge in MARCOING area. Completed new make print in CREVECOEUR	H.J.R.
		"	and transport completing repairs of bridge at L.23.G.0.8 and locks MARCOING. L.22.G.11 in MARCOING.	H.J.R.
		2 " " Engineering and recreational training	H.J.R.
	16.10.18		4 sections on Engineering and recreational training	H.J.R.
	17.10.18		As for 16.10.18. and also Lewis Gunnery.	H.J.R.
	18.10.18		No. 2. section proceeds to billets near MASNIERES; engaged on Patrols & repairs to bridge with transport and water points	H.J.R.
			Remainder of Company Training.	H.J.R.
	19.10.18		As for 18.10.18	H.J.R.
	20.10.18		Whole Company with transport moved to CANTANIERES	H.J.R.
	21.10.18		Company resting in CANTANIERES picking up No.1 section en route	H.J.R.
	22.10.18		Whole company with Transport moved to QUIEVY	H.J.R.
			No.2 section attached to 5th Inf. Brigade for work.	H.J.R.
			Half No.4 section with lodging material moved into SOLESMES	H.J.R.
	23.10.18		Remainder of company standing by	H.J.R.
			No.4 section Completed Tautmann bridge over river HARPIES in ROMERIES. W.21.d.39. and deviations leading Down	H.J.R.

WAR DIARY

INTELLIGENCE SUMMARY.
(Erase heading not required.)

Army Form C. 2118.

438TH (CHESHIRE) FIELD COMPANY, R.E.

OCTOBER 1918
SHEET No. 3

Instructions regarding War Diaries and Intelligence Summaries are contained in F. S. Regs., Part II. and the Staff Manual respectively. Title pages will be prepared in manuscript.

Place	Date	Hour	Summary of Events and Information	Remarks and references to Appendices
	24.10.18		3 Sections with transport in 2 reliefs working on bridge reconstruction in ROMERIES at W.21.d.38	H.J.R.
	25.10.18		Company with transport less 1 section moved to SOLESMES	H.J.R.
	26.10.18		3 Sections with transport in 2 reliefs working on bridge at W.21.d.38 Bridging equipment left behind at QUIEVY brought forward to SOLESMES	H.J.R.
	27.10.18		Company moved with transport to BUSSIERES near BEAUDIGNIES : No.2 Section and transport allowed O.y. from Brigade	H.J.R.
	28.10.18		Transport moved to Factory, CAPELLE No.2 Section working on improvement of BERMERAIN – RUESNES Road by day.	H.J.R.
	29.10.18		Nos 1,2 & 3 Sections working on improvement of BERMERAIN – RUESNES Road by day.	H.J.R.
			No.1 Section constructed Foot-bridge over River ECAILLON near BUSSIERES.	H.J.R.
			" 2 " Working on BERMERAIN – RUESNES Road	
			" 3 " Prepare pickets etc for track from RUESNES to BELLEVUE Farm.	
	30.10.18		4 Sections in details enployed on tracks and roads	H.J.R.
			Whole Company with transport moved to SOLESMES	
	31.10.18		Company with transport moved to BEVILLERS	H.J.R.

CASUALTIES

1. O.R. Died of Wounds
1. O.R. Wounded
D. O.R. Wounded "at duty."

Lt. T.M. COTTRELL. — was awarded M.C. First Awarded. R.O. No 1827 of 18.10.17

Authority: Third Army R.O. No 1827 of 18.10.17

John [Signature] Major R.E.(T)
O.C. 438th Cheshire Fld.Coy R.E.
31.10.18.

WAR DIARY

INTELLIGENCE SUMMARY.
(Erase heading not required.)

Army Form C. 2118.

438TH (CHESHIRE) FIELD COMPANY R.E.

NOVEMBER 1918.
SHEET No. 1.

V.8. 46

Place	Date	Hour	Summary of Events and Information	Remarks and references to Appendices
	1.11.18		Half-section of sappers erecting baths at BEVILLERS. Remainder of Company noting & mechanical training.	H.J.K.
	2.11.18		Half section Sappers controlling baths at BEVILLERS. Kit clean down and billet inspections. Remainder of company: handling of arms.	H.J.K.
	3.11.18		Church Parade	H.J.K.
	4.11.18		Whole company and transport moves to SOLESMES	H.J.K.
	5.11.18		Company standing by to move.	H.J.K.
	6.11.18		Company and transport moves to BELLEVUE Farm and HALT near RUESNES	H.J.K.
	7.11.18		3 Sections with transport worked by day on road repairs LE-QUESNOY - BAVAI Road. 1 erected hospital for field guns at R.II.C.52 near ORSINVAL	H.J.K.
	8.11.18		3 Sections with transport worked by day on road repairs LE-QUESNOY-BAVAI Road. 1 Section making Chateau FRASNOY suitable billets/offices fit for Div. H.Q.	H.J.K.
	9.11.18		Whole Company with transport (less Indian equipment moves to GOMMEGNIES)	H.J.K.
	10.11.18		4 Sections on road repairs with transport, vicinity of GOMMEGNIES	H.J.K.
	11.11.18		Whole company started on march to MAUBEUGE at 06.45 hours: Indian equipment brought from BELLEVUE FARM 4 sections on repairs at ARMISTICE with GERMANY at 07.50 hours orders	H.J.K.
	12.11.18		4 Sections on roads in vicinity of GOMMEGNIES	H.J.K.
	13.11.18		4 Sections with transport on roads in vicinity of GOMMEGNIES	H.J.K.
	14.11.18		2 Sections with transport on roads in vicinity of GOMMEGNIES	H.J.K.

Army Form C. 2118.

WAR DIARY
INTELLIGENCE SUMMARY.
(Erase heading not required.)

438th (CHESHIRE) FIELD COMPANY R.E.

NOVEMBER 1918
SHEET No. 2

Place	Date	Hour	Summary of Events and Information	Remarks and references to Appendices
	15.11.18		1 Section in Bivouac in vicinity of GOMMEGNIES. 3 Sections in Camp cleaning & painting vehicles: overhauling Equipment	W.7.28.
	16.11.18		4 Sections in Camp as for 15.11.18	W.3.21.
	17.11.18		As for 16.11.18	W.3.21.
	18.11.18		Company marched with 8th Inf. Bde. to NEUF-MESNIL and MAUBEUGE	W.11.28.
	19.11.18		Company resting and cleaning up.	W.7.28.
	20.11.18		Company marched with 8th Inf. Bde. to FERRIERE-LE-GRAND	W.7.28.
	21.11.18		do	W.7.28.
	22.11.18		4 Sections handling of arms and squad mounting.	W.11.28.
	23.11.18		4 Sections handling of arms and close order drill	W.11.28.
	24.11.18		As for 22.11.18	W.7.28.
	25.11.18		Company marched with 8th Inf. Bde. to MONTIGNIES	W.7.28.
	26.11.18		do to GOZEE	W.7.28.
	27.11.18		Company marched with 8th Inf. Bde. to SOMZEE	W.7.28.
	28.11.18		1 Section sent with draining mines in vicinity of THUIN and GOZEES	W.7.28.
	29.11.18		Company marched with 8th Inf. Bde. to FURNAUX	W.23.9.
	30.11.18		" " EVRE HAILLES	W.13.5.
			" " DORINNE	W.13.5.

HONOUR

L/Cpl WARING awarded LA CROIX DE GUERRE (French) Australian Division Routine Order 405. 1.11.18

John Showard Major R.E.(T)
O.C. 438 (Cheshire) Field Coy

WAR DIARY
INTELLIGENCE SUMMARY.
(Erase heading not required.)

Army Form C. 2118.

438TH (CHESHIRE) FIELD COMPANY, R.E.

DECEMBER 1918.
SHEET No. 1.

Instructions regarding War Diaries and Intelligence Summaries are contained in F. S. Regs., Part II. and the Staff Manual respectively. Title pages will be prepared in manuscript.

Place	Date	Hour	Summary of Events and Information	Remarks and references to Appendices
	1.12.18		Coy: at DORINNE. Resting and cleaning up	M.J.S.
	2.12.18		" " " Clean arm inspection and handing up arms.	(H.) J.S.
	3.12.18		" " " Handing of arms and close order drill	H.J.S.
	4.12.18		Coy: marched with 8th Inf. Bde. to SKEUVRE	H.J.S.
	5.12.18		" " " " MARESSE	H.J.S.
	6.12.18		" " " " MONVILLE	H.J.S.
	7.12.18		" " " " FISENNE	H.J.S.
	8.12.18		" " " " GRANDMENIL	H.J.S.
	9.12.18		" " " " FRAITURE	H.J.S.
	10.12.18		Coy: at FRAITURE. Resting and cleaning up.	H.J.S.
	11.12.18		Coy: marched with 8th Inf. Bde. to PETITE LANGLIER.	H.J.S.
	12.12.18		" " " " BEHO.	H.J.S.
	13.12.18		" " " " NEUN DORF. Entered GERMANY on this day.	H.J.S.
	14.12.18		" " " " ANDLER.	H.J.S.
	15.12.18		" " " " HALLSCHLAG	H.J.S.
	16.12.18		" " " " MULHEIM (near BLANKENHEIM)	H.J.S.
	17.12.18		" " " " EICHERSCHEID	H.J.S.
	18.12.18		" " " " SATZVEY	H.J.S.
	19.12.18		" " " " MUDDERSHEIM	H.J.S.
	20.12.18		" " independently to DUREN.	H.J.S.
DUREN	21.12.18		Clean arm inspection and cleaning vehicles	H.J.S.
	22.12.18		Changing billets in barracks and front latrines	H.J.S.
	23.12.18		Erecting Tarpaulin latrines and re-erecting latrines	H.J.S.
	24.12.18		Cultivating latrines and parking wagons.	H.J.S.
	25-31.12.18		Whole Coy. on Barrack Improvements in armoury.	H.J.S.

John Rhead Major R.E. (T)
O.C. 438. (Cheshire) Field Coy.

Army Form C. 2118.

WAR DIARY
or
INTELLIGENCE SUMMARY.
(Erase heading not required.)

430TH (CHESHIRE) FIELD COMPANY, R.E.

JANUARY 1919

Vol 48

Place	Date	Hour	Summary of Events and Information	Remarks and references to Appendices
DUREN GERMANY	1.1.19 to 31.1.19		<u>Daily Routine</u> ½ hour each morning devoted to training - drill, physical exercises etc 3½ " at work on Barrack improvements & education afternoons free for games and sport evenings - concerts & other entertainment	H.P.2.
			<u>CASUALTIES</u> No 446131 Sergeant RIXON E awarded M.S.M. London Gazette January 1919. W.O. 16.1.19.	H.P.2.

Harry B Smiley Capt. R.E.(T)
A/o.c. 438 (Cheshire) Field Coy.
31.1.19.

Army Form C. 2118

438TH (CHESHIRE) FIELD COMPANY, R.E.

WAR DIARY
INTELLIGENCE SUMMARY.
(Erase heading not required.)

FEBRUARY 1919

Place	Date	Hour	Summary of Events and Information	Remarks and references to Appendices
DUREN GERMANY	1st to 28th	09.00 to 09.30	Company drill, handling of arms, saluting & close order drill etc.	H.Q.
		09.30		H.Q.
		09.20 to 12.00	All others employed in Barrack Improvements and works for out lying units	H.Q. H.Q.
			Officers detailed to services etc. according to their vocation	H.Q. H.Q.
			CASUALTIES	
			Lt. G.T. COTTERELL. Struck off strength as from 25.1.19 whilst on leave in England	H.Q.
			Lt. G.L.E. STEELEY. To Hospital 17.2.19.	H.Q.
			2Lt. T.M. COTTRELL M.C. Struck off strength as from 26.1.19 on proceeding to [?]appointment as Adjutant. R.E. H.Q.R.E. 29th Division.	H.Q.

(Signed) J.T. Crumley
Capt. OE(?)
No. 438 (Cheshire) Field Co. R.E.(?)
28.2.19

Army Form C. 2118.

438TH (CHESHIRE) FIELD COMPANY, R.E.

MARCH 1919.

SHEET No 1

WAR DIARY
INTELLIGENCE SUMMARY.
(Erase heading not required.)

Instructions regarding War Diaries and Intelligence Summaries are contained in F.S. Regs., Part II. and the Staff Manual respectively. Title pages will be prepared in manuscript.

Place	Date	Hour	Summary of Events and Information	Remarks and references to Appendices
GERMANY				
DUREN	1/3/19		Packing / Vehicle preparations for move to Cologne	aps
DUREN	2/3/19	09.00	Company moves independently to KERPEN. Arrives at 12.40 hrs 2/3/19	aps
KERPEN	3/3/19	09.00	Company proceeds to COLOGNE (BRAUNSFELD) Arrives at 12.55 hrs 3/3/19	aps
COLOGNE (BRAUNSFELD)	4/3/15 to	09.00 to 16.00	Close order Drill. Handling of arms etc	aps
	16th	10.00 to 12.30	Work on Billet Improvements and work in out-lying Units	aps
			Afternoon devoted to Games etc	aps
			Evenings to other Recreations.	aps
COLOGNE (BRAUNSFELD)	17th to 31st	09.00 to 10.00	Company Drill etc.	aps
		10.00 to 12.30	Work on Billet Improvements and work in out-lying Units.	aps
		14.00 to 16.20	Saturday & Sunday Afternoons devoted to Games Evenings to other Recreations	aps
	30th	10.15	The Company was present in Div RE at RE Workshops in order that G.O.C 3rd Div might pay Good bye to 56 Fd Coy RE and all men awaiting demobilization. The Officers present were. Major E.L. Martin MC RE, MC C.E.F. Turner RE, MC B.P. Weir RE, Lt. G.L. Steeley RE, Lt. E.B. Bellingfort RE, Lt. H.A. Bazley RE, 2/Lt R.W. Hutchens RE	aps

WAR DIARY

Army Form C. 2118.

488th (Cheshire) Field Company, R.E.

MARCH 1919 SHEET No 2

Place	Date	Hour	Summary of Events and Information	Remarks and references to Appendices
GERMANY COLOGNE			CASUALTIES	
			2Lt. E.L. Richardson R.E. Taken on Strength 3/3/19	AR20
			2Lt. R. McCrea. R.E. Struck off Strength 25/3/19.	AR20
			Lt. H.A. Bazley R.E. To Hospital 4/3/19.	AR20
			2Lt. C.E.F. Turner R.E. Taken on Strength 10/3/19.	AR20
			2Lt. E.A. Bellinger R.E. Taken on Strength 10/3/19.	AR20
			Lt. G.L.E. Steeley R.E. Taken on Strength 21/3/19.	AR20
			Lt. A/Capt H.J.F. Gourley. R.E. Rejoins Coy from Sick Leave 24/3/19 appointed a/Major 22/3/19 Struck off Strength 26/3/19.	AR20
			Major E.L. Martin M.C. R.E. Resumes Command from 22/3/19.	AR20
			Cpl Sharrock. awarded Bar to Military Medal. D.R.O. 87. A/04 28/2/19.	AR20

R Turner MAJOR R.E.
O.C. 438 F.S Coy. R.E.

Army Form C. 2118

WAR DIARY
or
INTELLIGENCE SUMMARY
(Erase heading not required.)

No. 453th (QUEENSLAND) FIELD COMPANY, R.E.

APRIL 1919

Place	Date	Hour	Summary of Events and Information	Remarks and references to Appendices
COLOGNE (BRAUNSFELD) GERMANY	1st to 4th	08:00 to 16:30	Company working 6 hours daily on Barrack Improvements to 2nd & 3rd NORTHERN BDES.	a/fw
	5th	—	Company moves to RIEHL (COLOGNE)	a/fw
RIEHL	6th to 30th		Daily Routine as above.	a/fw
	19th		Major General Ruckard. Chief Engineer Army of the Rhine. inspected Billets and Complimented the Company on the smartness of the Guard	a/fw
			CASUALTIES	
			Lt H.D. MAJOR MONOCHIE MC RE. Taken on strength 26.3.19. (From 3rd Fd Squadron R.E.) (on leave from 27.3.19)	a/fw
			Lt G.L.E. STEELEY R.E. Struck off Strength 30.3.19. (to 56 Fd Coy R.E.)	a/fw
			2Lt A.W. CUNLIFFE R.E. Taken on strength 3.4.19. from 56 Fd Coy R.E.	a/fw
			2Lt W.D.G. HUGHES R.E. Taken on strength 3.4.19. from 56 Fd Coy R.E.	a/fw
			Lt H. KEMSLEY R.E. Struck off strength 4.4.19. (to 1st Field Squadron R.E.)	a/fw
			2Lt A.W. CUNLIFFE R.E. attached to H.Q. R.E. Northern Divn. as O/C R.E. Workshops 15.4.19.	a/fw
			MAJOR E.L. MARTIN MC. RE assumes command of Northern Divisional RE. from 15.4.19.	a/fw
			CAPT W.G. EVANS R.E. Taken on strength 10.4.17. (From 301st Fd Coy R.E.)	c/fw
			CAPT W. & EVANS R.E. assumes command from 15.4.19.	a/fw
			2/Lt C.E.F. TURNER R.E. Struck off strength from 16.4.19. (to 2nd Fd Survey Coy R.E.)	a/fw
			2Lt E.A. BELLINGER R.E. on Leave 20.4.19.	a/fw
			2Lt W.D.G. HUGHES R.E. From Leave 21.4.19.	a/fw
			2/Lt W.D.G. HUGHES R.E. to Hospital 27.4.19.	a/fw
			Lt H.D. MAJONOCHIE RE. From Leave 29.4.19.	a/fw

J. Howard Major R.E.
O.C. 438 Field Coy R.E.
30/4/19.

Army Form C. 2118.

WAR DIARY
or
INTELLIGENCE SUMMARY.
(Erase heading not required.)

Page 1.

483rd
CONFERENCE
FIELD COMPANY R.E.

MAY 1919.

Place	Date	Hour	Summary of Events and Information	Remarks and references to Appendices
RIEHL COLOGNE	1st.		Daily Routine, work on Billets & barrack improvements for 2nd & 3rd Northern Inf. Bde. throughout month of May.	aPw
	6th.		Lt. E.A. BERINGER R.E. rejoined from leave.	aPw
	7th.		Lt. W.D.P. HUGHES R.E. from hospital	aPw
	8th.		REVIEW BY THE DUKE OF CONNAUGHT. — (NORTHERN DIV. REVIEW)	aPw
	10th.		INSPECTION OF TRANSPORT. BY. C.R.E. Northern Dis.	aPw
	17th.		INSPECTION OF TRANSPORT BY. C.R.E. Northern Div	aPw
	19th		Major E.L. MARTIN. M.C. R.E. on leave to FRANCE. (10 days)	aPw
	19th.		CAPT. W.A. EVANS R.E. assumes command in Major Martin's absence.	aPw
	22nd		Lieut H.D. MACONOCHIE. M.C. R.E. attached to C.R.E. as Adjutant R.E.	aPw
	30th		C.R.E. inspected Company in full marching order. Major E.L. Martin, M.C. R.E. returned from leave & proceeded command of Company.	aPw

LEAVE — Officers — 2
O.R. — 18

Casualties.

Army Form C. 2118.

WAR DIARY
INTELLIGENCE SUMMARY

(Erase heading not required.)

438TH (CHESHIRE) FIELD COMPANY, R.E.

MAY, 1919

Page 2

Instructions regarding War Diaries and Intelligence Summaries are contained in F. S. Regs., Part II. and the Staff Manual respectively. Title pages will be prepared in manuscript.

Place	Date	Hour	Summary of Events and Information	Remarks and references to Appendices
RIEHL, COLOGNE.	May 1919		Casualties (cont'd) Demobilised - from unit - 1 on leave - 5 To Hospital - 2 Reinforcements - 16	

G.J. Martin Maj. R.E.
O.C. 436th Fld Coy R.E.
31/5/19

Army Form C. 2118.

Page I.

WAR DIARY
INTELLIGENCE SUMMARY

(Erase heading not required.)

438TH (CHESHIRE) FIELD COMPANY R.E.

July 1919

Place	Date	Hour	Summary of Events and Information	Remarks and references to Appendices
RIEHL COLOGNE	1st		Daily waiting work on Bielets & Langels improvements for 2nd & 3rd Panthers Sect. Bde transport: repairs & pull up keep ist and 2nd.	80/2 80/2
	2nd		Company returned from WERMELSKIRCHEN.	80/6
	3rd		Major Martin M.C.R.E. on leave to France (14 days)	80/6
	7th		General Holiday in honour of Peace.	80/6
			F.G.C.M. - Lieut Davis J.	80/6
			Lt MACONOCHIE R.E. to C.R.E. as A/ADJT.	80/6
	10th		F.G.C.M. Lieut Davis J. promoted OBE reduced to ranks + 30 days Pay R.W.	80/6
	11th		I.O.R. ewets posted to 529 Co.	80/6
	12th		I.O.R. to U.K. for demobilisation	80/6
	16th		MAJOR E.L. MARTIN M.C. R.E. returned from leave.	80/6
	17th		Lt. HUGHES to II CORPS H.Q. as fixed engineer.	80/6
	18th		Lt. A.H.MADDY joined from 529 Field. Co. R.E. - I.O.R. base parties (3)	80/6 80/6
	19th		Peace Day general holiday.	80/6
	20th		I.O.R. ewets posted to 3rd Field Co. R.E.	80/6

Army Form C. 2118.

WAR DIARY
INTELLIGENCE SUMMARY
(Erase heading not required.)

438TH (CHESHIRE) FIELD COMPANY, R.E.

JULY 1919

Place	Date	Hour	Summary of Events and Information	Remarks and references to Appendices
RIEHL	21st		1 O.R. to hospital	80/8
	22nd		1 O.R. Cross posted from 231 Co R.E.	80/9
COLOGNE	23rd		Lt. MACONOCHIE returned from C.R.E.	80/10
	24th			80/11
			1 O.R. WEIRS & MADDY to U.K. for demobilization also 1 O.R.	80/12
	27th		Capt W.Q. EVANS to U.K. on leave	80/10
			H/Capt CUNLIFFE arr posted to 231 Co R.E.	80/18
	29th		MAJOR E.K. MARTIN (M.C.) R.E. ACTING C.R.E.	80/6
	31st		1 O.R. Bacon posted to 231 Co R.E.	80/12
			Casualties	
			Leave – Officers 2 Reinforcements Officers 1	80/8
			O.Rs. 65 O.R. —	80/10
			Hospital Officers 1 Invalid Officers 2	80/6
			O.Rs. 4 O.Rs. —	80/13

E.A. Beringer ? Lt. R.E.
A/O.C. 438 Field Co R.E.

Army Form C. 2118.

WAR DIARY
INTELLIGENCE SUMMARY
(Erase heading not required.)

[433RD CHESHIRE FIELD COMPANY R.E.]

July 1919

Place	Date	Hour	Summary of Events and Information	Remarks and references to Appendices
RIEHL COLOGNE	1st		Daily routine work in billets & barracks. Improvements for transport mounted. 1st & 3rd further buildings put into use. 1st and 3rd	SO/3 SO/2
	2nd		Company returned from WERMELSKIRCHEN	SO/6
	3rd		Major F.M. MARTIN M.C. R.E. on leave to France (in Army)	SO/6
	7th		General holiday in honour of Peace	SO/6
	9th		F.G.C.M. - Lieut Davis J.	SO/6
			Lt MACONOCHIE R.E. to C.R.E. ao 9/7/21st.	
	10th		F.G.C.M. Lieut Davis J. promulgated returned to duties & 30 days Py R.U.	SO/6
	11th		O.R. evens (battn) to 529 Co.	SO/6
	12th		I.O.R. to U.K. for demobilisation	SO/6
	16th		MAJOR F.L. MARTIN M.C. R.E. returned from leave.	SO/6
	17th		Lt HUGHES to II CORPS H.Q. on Peace Engineer.	SO/6
	15th		T.A.A. MADDY	SO/6
	19th		Joined from 529 Fd. Co. R.E. - 1 OR. on posting to	SO/6
	20th		Peace Bn Reinf Hernry's Fd. Co. R.E.	SO/6 / (251 Fd.oo.R.E.)

Army Form C. 2118

WAR DIARY

INTELLIGENCE SUMMARY.
(Erase heading not required.)

JULY 1919

Instructions regarding War Diaries and Intelligence Summaries are contained in F. S. Regs., Part II. and the Staff Manual respectively. Title pages will be prepared in manuscript.

[Stamp: 438TH (COLOGNE) FIELD COMPANY, R.E.]

Place	Date	Hour	Summary of Events and Information	Remarks and references to Appendices
BILLETS COLOGNE	22nd		1 O.R. to Hospital	80/18 80/13
	23rd		1 O.R. Cross posted from 231 Co R.E.	80/13
	24th		Lt Macnochie returns from C.R.E.	80/13
	27th		Lts. Weirs & Maddy to U.K. for Demobilization also 1 O.R	70/17 80/13
			Capt W.Q. Evans to U.K. on leave	80/13
	29th		Lt Cunliffe Cross posted to 231 Co R.E.	80/13
			Major E.L. Martin (N)C.R.E. ACTING C.R.E	80/13
	31st		1 O.R. Cross posted to 231 Co. R.E.	80/18 80/13
			Casualties	
			Leave — Officers 2 Reinforcements Officers 1	80/18 80/13
			O.R. 65 O.R.	
			Hospital Officer 1 Unroll'd Officer 2	80/18 80/13
			O.R. 4 O.R. 2	

E.J. Beainf Lt R.E.
A/O.C. 438th Field Co R.E.

Army Form C. 2118

WAR DIARY
or
INTELLIGENCE SUMMARY.

(Erase heading not required.)

438TH (CHESHIRE) FIELD COMPANY R.E.

August 1919

Place	Date	Hour	Summary of Events and Information	Remarks and references to Appendices
Raihl	August 4th		Lt Macrochie M.C. R.E. proceeded on leave to U.K.	—
	6th		Major E.L. Martin M.C. R.E. to Hospital, † Lt E.A. Bellanger, assumed Command	—
Cologne	11th		Major E.L. Martin M.C. R.E. returned from Hospital & resumed Command M.C. R.E. on leave.	—
	18th		Review of Coy. transport & 21 O.R. with VI Corps troops RE by Army Council Exercise Platz, Mulheim.	—
	19th		Lt Macrochie M.C. R.E. on leave.	—
	21st		⇥ Lt E.A. Bellanger R.E. proceeded on leave	—
	23rd		Lt Macrochie M.C. R.E. to O.C. R.E. to take over Adjutant	—
	31st		Social evening for Company.	—
			Leave {Officers – 2. Transfers – 2 to Egypt.	—
			{O.R. – 30. Invalided – O.R. – 1	—
			Hospital {Officer – 1 Mulus – 85 VI Corps tps A.C.C.	—
			{O.R. – 10	—
			Reinforcements O.R. – 1.	—

E.L. Martin Maj. R.E.
O.C. 438th Fld. Cy. R.E.

A 2531 Art. W 4973/M687 750,000 8/16 D. D. & L. Ltd. Forms/C.2118/13.

Army Form C. 2118.

WAR DIARY
or
INTELLIGENCE SUMMARY.

(Erase heading not required.)

Instructions regarding War Diaries and Intelligence Summaries are contained in F. S. Regs., Part II. and the Staff Manual respectively. Title pages will be prepared in manuscript.

438 (CHESHIRE) FIELD COMPANY R.E.

September 1919

Place	Date	Hour	Summary of Events and Information	Remarks and references to Appendices
Rielly	Sept. 5		2ⁿᵈ Lt. E. A. Billings returned from leave	W.D.
Cologne	19		2ⁿᵈ Lt. E. A. Billings appointed Lieutenant, auth. Lond. Gaz. 19/9/19 & antedated to 21/8/1918	W.D.
	21		Maj. E. L. Martin, M.C. R.E., proceeded on leave to France & Capt. W.W. Irons M.C., R.E., assumed command.	W.D.
			Summary:-	
			Leave:- Officers — 1.	
			O. R's. — 11.	
			Hospital:- O.R. — 1 to Bashtik	W.D.
			O.R. — 1 from "	
			Horses:- 1 rider evacuated to N.11. Mobile Vet. Sect.	
			5. "S" horses to Animals Collecting Camp.	
			Re-enlistments:- O.R. — 1. (Proceeded on 2 months furlough	W.D.
			(S.W.R).	
			Demobilisation:-	
			O.R. — 70. (15 O.R. returned to unit on the 26ᵗʰ as no Demobilisation was carried out by D Railway Station in England.)	W.D.

W.W. Irons Capt. R.E.
O.C. 438 Field Cy. R.E.

Army Form C. 2118.

WAR DIARY
or
INTELLIGENCE SUMMARY.
(Erase heading not required.)

438TH (CHESHIRE) FIELD COMPANY R.E.

October 1919

Place	Date	Hour	Summary of Events and Information	Remarks and references to Appendices
RIEHL COLOGNE	1st to 30th		Company employed on work.	
	8th		Major E. L. Martin M.C. R.E. rejoined from leave	
	15th		Capt. W. A. Evans M.C. R.E. transferred to the 219th Field Co R.E.	
	16th		2/Lt. R. H. Muirhead granted leave to U.K.	
	23rd		All wagons & wagon equipment to MERHEIM.	
	29th		2/Lt. E. A. Beevers R.E. transferred to 219th Field Co R.E.	
	30th		Company disbanded — Capt. F. Naithwaite R.E., A/Q.M.S. Tranmere W.M. R.E., A/1 Cpl. Lee T. R.E. detailed to wind record home.	

E. L. Martin Major R.E.
O.C. 438th Field Co., R.E.